T0062858

The
WISER-MOUSE LEGACY

Other books by author

Little Boy Wild—2006
www.littleboywild.com

The
WISER-MOUSE LEGACY

On Being An Authentic Christian!

DEREK V. EVERARD

WESTBOW
PRESS
A DIVISION OF THOMAS NELSON

Unless otherwise noted, scripture taken from the New King James Version.
Copyright 1979, 1980, 1982 by Thomas Nelson, inc.
Used by permission. All rights reserved.

WestBow Press books may be ordered through booksellers or by contacting:

WestBow Press
A Division of Thomas Nelson
1663 Liberty Drive
Bloomington, IN 47403
www.westbowpress.com
1-(866) 928-1240

ISBN: 978-1-4497-4900-2 (sc)
ISBN: 978-1-4497-4899-9 (e)

Library of Congress Control Number: 2012907170

Printed in the United States of America

WestBow Press rev. date: 5/16/2014

The Wiser-Mouse Legacy

"There is one body, and one Spirit, just as you were called in one hope of your calling; one Lord, one faith, one baptism; one God and Father of all, who is above all, and through all, and in you all."

NKJV (Ephesians 4:4-6).

E-Mail: authentic_christianity@telus.net
www.wiser-mouse.com

CONTENTS

AUTHOR'S NOTES AND ACKNOWLEDGEMENTS

Throughout this journey to spiritual maturity numerous insights were illuminated by the lamps of wisdom, (and of ignorance), by those who preceded me. Great poets, researchers, writers, psychologists, philosophers, scientists, Bible scholars, and the purveyors of man-made religions, all contributed their versions of reality to these sometimes confusing vortices of wisdom.

All of these inputs called for the development of special awareness in the comprehension of that which we hear, see, read or experience. Our need is to greatly enhance our spiritual-discernment. We will encounter clouds of unknowing, where that which is false is accepted by millions as "truth". The indwelling truth of the living Word is a gift of the Holy Spirit.

I sincerely thank all my fellow-humans who gifted me with gems of truth. Many contributed to the comprehension that I treasure today. I have become a selective composite of their visions. The wisdom retained from these inputs was nurtured from the indwelling of the Holy Spirit. He separated truth from error through gentle and loving guidance, which overcame my sins of rebellion and self-righteous reasoning. I discovered that human-based logic and spiritual understanding occupy two quite different dimensions.

Many, many thanks go to Shendra Hanney for her unswerving dedication to her proven editing talents, including monitoring the text for relevancy, flow and elegance. Additionally, she contributed valuable spiritual insight. Shendra's astute observations occasionally included changing of words or re-phrasing of sentences.

At times this caused me to become quite defensive. I discovered that when someone enters into the birthing-process of a book, it is equivalent to that of a stranger intruding on the birthing scenario of a little grizzly cub!

However, the editing and proof-reading of this small volume was a sheer delight that we both enjoyed. A tribute to our attitudinal maturity was that a lot of give-and-take was incurred. The results were that deletions, toning down, and other changes were effected without difficulty.

Heartfelt thanks go to trusted and patient friend Jacob Wiebe, for combing our text with eyes of spiritual discernment. This was so welcome and necessary to ensure that our doctrine of Authentic Christianity in no way deviated from Biblical spiritual truths.

A special thanks to Dot Lines for her splendid photo of *Wiser-Mouse* which appears on our front cover. It was drawn from her many photo resources of Yellow-Necked mice. Dot Lines is known world-wide for her excellence in U.K. wildlife photography in addition to her work on African wildlife.

The *Wiser-Mouse Legacy* was not born out of a desire to write a book. There is no ego-involvement in the entire volume. It was a Christian response to being transparent and obedient, the purpose of which was to be definitive in my current understanding of God, and indeed all of Christianity. In so doing, I humbly acknowledge that the thoughts of Man can never be entirely free of error.

There are those who may perceive this text on current Christianity as a low-level diatribe. In reality, this exploration is somewhat similar to an aircraft engineer performing a diagnostic study of a failed aircraft engine. Any such report will be subject to the experience of the investigating engineer. The parts are examined and causal facts are identified. Observations and evidence of status are simply documented, and solutions are formulated for future design.

Still others of high intelligence and education will relegate spiritual-insight to pure hallucination. However, this may be limited to those whose world-interpretation is based only in the five senses and logic. These beings may not as yet have perceived, or yielded, to the spiritual dimension in which authentic Christianity is contained.

Our text is analogous to that of providing a guide for travellers seeking a flight-path through what I see as intense spiritual darkness. Although it was not my original intent, the text became a "spiritual GPS unit" for those who recognize the need to locate themselves, change direction, or be equipped to enter the world to come.

You are invited to explore these insights. They were gifted me through the Holy Spirit for use by others. However, I would not have you believe this is a special "Holy" book. The narrations of the earthly-man and those of the spiritual-man are clearly evident.

No ownership of ideas is implied, nor any claims to originality, as that which has been conceived is as old as the Bible. This little volume is primarily a commitment to spiritual obedience. There were no options. It was an act of empowerment through the Holy Scriptures under the direction of the Holy Spirit.

In its entirety, this little volume is merely a gifted instrument through which our heavenly Father is glorified. Amen.

CHAPTER ONE

The *Wiser-Mouse Legacy* is primarily an exploration of "Authentic Christianity". It relates entirely to our journey on Earth, which is at the core of our spiritual ascension. However, the term journey is quite inadequate, as a "journey" is simply travelling from one point to another. Whereas, what we are embarking upon could rightly be described as an odyssey, as in *Homer's Odyssey*.

This is an adventure into new vistas of consciousness. It embraces the mainstream elements of many spiritual journeys as well as the Christian one. No attempt has been made to hide the truth of our humanness behind a façade of niceness, in order to please the reader. This would merely lull him further into the blissful sleeping state of the "living dead".

It is a long voyage of exploration marked with many changes in spirit, soul, and body over lengthy periods of time. Life and death adventures with unprecedented personal growth always accompany one's spiritual ascension. This odyssey reveals a "now" level of consciousness to be attained. This *now* is vertical to *time*. It well may challenge the status quo of those who still "sleep like pebbles in the stream of time".

We commence this adventure in a wonderful wilderness location in British Columbia. It is a warm fall day with a cloudless blue sky. The setting is a large green meadow yellow with dandelion faces. The log buildings and cabins are surrounded by forest. A light fall breeze prevails as the trees lazily shed their red and yellow leaves.

The woodlands blend as well as contrast with their dark green stands of firs and cedars. There is an overall aura of expectancy, perhaps enchantment. Anything can happen and probably will! This is that air of anticipatory magic that pervades such a scene, and slowly triggers within one involuntary words of praise to our heavenly Father. A raven calls, magpies chatter, and a small, fast creek burbles by the trail. It reveals tracks of little hoof marks where the deer come down to drink.

One's eye is urged to accept the invitation to explore the trails that disappear at the forest's edge. When dusk falls heralding the cool of a starry night, one images a cozy log fire and the warm presence of those who seek the truth of how life should be lived.

I had never previously had an opportunity to be a part of a retreat group, due to extensive business travel, and no firm church affiliation at home base. As a lay Christian, in these travels I was often gifted the opportunity to participate in local Bible studies.

Now, I experienced a feeling of elation at the prospect of interacting with pastors, elders, and many other dedicated fellow Christians in a male weekend retreat. Within me was a hunger for definitive answers to many questions relating to what the scriptures taught, and what I had experienced in actual Christian Protestant practise.

Further, I planned to explore what I considered to be the obvious symptoms of "impotent" Christianity, as it is now so commonly practiced. I needed to arrive at attainable scriptural solutions to these spiritual observations.

Then, scrambling up a steep slope to a vantage point for viewing wildlife, it happened! As sudden as the brilliant flash of bluebird wings in the early spring, a beautiful and

2

remarkable inspiration descended upon me! It was no doubt triggered by the wilderness setting, the lonely cabins, and the sublime solitude.

I envisioned weaving into the text a series of spiritual quotes that I had discovered quite by chance a number of years ago. I had always referred to these intriguing scribbles as the *Lost Notebooks of Wiser-Mouse*. It was then a great temptation to kick off our treatise with: "Once upon a time ... a little mouse told me!"

This happenstance resulted from an extended two week hike in the west of England, a kind of walkabout to "find myself", during which I was overtaken by a monsoon-type of unrelenting rainfall. It was then that I had blindly stumbled upon a deserted sheep herder's cottage nestled on the edge of some thick woods.

"Any port in a storm", I muttered upon entering, wedging the door shut against the onslaught. I was quickly able to get a fire going in the old stone fireplace. First it was smoky, and then worked into the roaring hot crackling fire I so much needed. Shivering with cold, and soaked to the skin; I rigged some clothes lines, stripped off, and basked in the wonderful heat. In one corner of the room was an old bale of hay which I cut open and spread out to serve as a mattress and reposing place. It was the type of hay that is fine and silky soft.

Later, revived by the heat, I took to padding around the old cottage to see what I may find. In the upstairs room, much to my surprise, I discovered some scattered notebooks partially hidden by a wooden crate that had contained sheep dip; and which later had probably served as a desk. A broken paraffin lamp lay on this desk, and a five gallon pail still survived as a seat.

My eyes became riveted on the notebooks which were covered with droppings from old swallow nests, dead flies, and deserted spider webs. Although they were scuffed and muddy with tiny paw tracks, yellowed with age, and partially chewed, the writings were still decipherable.

Most intriguing of all was that they were crudely signed as *"Wiser-Mouse"*. Overwhelmed with excitement, I returned to the heat of the fireplace. There, by firelight I was able to discern among the damp pages, two poems, and a host of other randomly scrawled papers of a spiritual nature.

Searching among the notes to find out why the writer had signed his work as *"Wiser-Mouse"*, I studiously examined every note that I had so carefully salvaged, but to no avail. However, I did suspect a mouse had something to do with it, if only based on the squeaking and scurrying within the walls!

With backpack unloaded, and supper stewing on a thick bed of red coals, I relaxed among the dancing shadows to carefully dry out the curious writings. The strange little rustlings and scampering of small paws did not abate. I was warm, happy, and surrounded by my woodland friends.

After taking a nip of Harvey's Bristol Cream along with my baked beans and Hovis loaf, I found an envelope that contained what appeared to be a self-portrait of the writer. A portrait artist he was not! But as I gazed at the sketch I perceived a small creature perched on his left shoulder.

It was a mouse, bright eyed and exquisite in every detail right to the tiniest whisker! I allowed that his eyes seemed to convey sacred knowledge. Thusly, recognition of the *mouse-connection* began to fall into place!

Much of my early life experience was that of cruel rejection, physical, sexual and psychological abuse, as well as being isolated from other humans; an extreme situation.

Under such bizarre circumstances, one not only develops a boundless imaginative world of a *different reality*; but one actually converses with real wild creatures. In living with the animals, one experiences an exquisite beauty and peace in their unconditional acceptance of other friendly types of beings.

The treasured friendship of a wild mouse surely warms the heart of one who has escaped the values of man. I could readily envision that while the lonely shepherd-writer and his little whiskered friend shared his dry bread and cheese; he also shared his spiritual wisdom. In this surreal relationship, he undoubtedly communed with this wise little creature; receiving mystical mouse affirmations from his quotes. Maybe that is why he signed his notes as *"Wiser-Mouse"?* We'll never know!

I had never made a study of these wee creatures, but this "mousey" was not a dormouse, nor an ordinary field-mouse. The artist had given him larger than usual ears, a longer tail, and what appeared to be a lighter ruff around the neck. On the chest of this beautiful little animal was a tiny brown star. Later research showed the *Wiser-Mouse* sketch to be that of a Yellow-Necked mouse. However, there was no brown star. On my visit I encountered only the wood mice.

During supper, I shared my heavy Hovis brown bread with the curious little creatures; while delighting in their various eating antics. One of them even nibbled bread from my fingers! After my repast, I stoked up the fire, and read a few *Wiser-Mouse* quotes. Allowing myself to be lost in sacred reverie, it seemed that I had become a living reality from the past.

That night, the *Lost Notebooks of Wiser-Mouse* created an aura of woodland magic. They captured my imagination. Meantime, the drenching cold rain swept in from across the moors to beat savagely against the old cottage. All night long, and especially when the light and heat from the fire had subsided, the friendly little wood mice scampered about.

When finally I fell asleep in my sleeping bag, I could feel tiny feet and bodies running over me. At dawn, on donning dry clothes again; I set up a mouse feast breakfast banquet of the remaining Hovis slices. For the kingdom of the mice, it was a treat that I suspected would never be repeated!

Later, at home base, I encountered difficulty in deciphering some of the writings due to smudging and dampness damage; but in the main I succeeded. Most amazing of all, was that when I consciously relaxed in the Spirit, it was as if *Wiser-Mouse* were perched on *my* left shoulder! It occurred to me that the truths, beauty, and spiritual wisdom contained in the shepherd's *Lost Notebooks,* could only have originated with the Holy Spirit.

Maybe the writer was a wise and advanced spiritual being. It is also possible that the uncluttered mind of a human in solitude, a lone shepherd in the hills, may experience forms of spiritual ascension unknown to the common man. The truth is probably that we are too caught up in the bustle of what is known as *living*, to ever encounter the realms of spirituality that need to be central in our lives.

As a result of this adventure, our text is interspersed with the legacy of the *"Wiser-Mouse"* quotes. Their undeniable wisdom, as they move into the twenty-first century are timeless! A portrait of *"Wiser-Mouse"* appears on our front cover. The entire series of "Mouse-Quotes" are included in the text!

In the meantime, lost in reverie, I spoke my thoughts aloud as I tramped through the bush delighting in the warm fall sun. When two white-tail deer looked up from their nibbling, and viewed me as just another forest creature, the day felt natural, relaxed and complete.

At this retreat, I planned to question the other participants on the critical matter of understanding the difference between the practise of authentic Christian churches, and those perceived by me to be Christian religious cults. Previously, I had asked others: "Why do your friends, whom you describe as 'wonderful Christian people', have an ongoing relationship with a known pseudo-Christian cult?" Replies to this question were usually: "Although other religions and their teachings may differ in significant ways, we still believe our friends to be wonderful Christians."

In practice, these people appear to have become unwitting innocent deviants, who have been led astray by false doctrine. Their assemblies fail in obvious ways to adhere to the Holy Scriptures. So, I wondered, what gives?

One cannot be scriptural while mixing truth with error. An old analogy says that being partially pregnant is a misnomer. We either are, or we are not!

We cannot be scriptural Christians that adhere to the Word in our Bibles, *and*, be consorting with evil forces at the same time. (Evil is that which is contrary to the Holy Scriptures and the commands of God).

False forms of Christianity turn the spiritual teachings of Jesus into soul-based wishful thinking, and impossible dreams. Too frequently we are confronted with spiritual facades disguised as truth. They rob us of many blessings.

Another question for the retreat members that became stuck in the forefront of my mind, was the matter of spiritual correctness; such as in relation to those who prayed directly to Jesus, which is not biblical, rather than praying to the Father in the name of Jesus. I have always regarded this oblique interpretation as being deviant and disturbing.

The general response to this enquiry seemed to be: "Well, it's the Trinity, it's all the same thing." The question was regarded as elementary, and of no consequence. No definitive answers were forthcoming.

It appears that Christians have quite a disarray of unity in comprehension of spiritual words. Among these are grace, doctrine, hope, belief, faith, and so forth. For many years I have been aware of these disparate differences of interpretation in Christian terms of reference.

A simple example is when assemblies are exhorted to "pray in faith". There are many who after years of Christian church attendance, simply have no concept of its true meaning. Faith is usually interpreted only as a belief in a particular church affiliation.

It also appears that many Christians are quite unclear on numerous matters of doctrine; or even what doctrine is. I needed to know the answer to the most basic question of all: *"Do we, or do we not, follow the exact words of the Holy Scriptures?"*

Are we all due for a lifesaving reality check? Just where do we stand? We need to face up to our own version of spiritual and scriptural reality!

It is often quoted that: "Christians don't follow signs, signs follow Christians." Also, biblically: "And these signs will follow those who believe. In My name they will cast out demons;

they will speak in new tongues; they will take up serpents; and if they drink anything deadly, it will by no means hurt them, they will lay hands on the sick, and they will recover." (Mark 16:17).

We see no *signs* forthcoming, and neither do we appear to expect any. "So where do we go from here?" I asked a noisy squirrel as he continued his unabated scolding. Finally, he flicked his tail and flowed across to another tree.

We Christians need to ask cutting-edge questions, such as: "Why are we here in a church assembly? Is it just for the time-consuming pleasantries that we call "fellowship"? Just what are our personal Christian priorities? Have we ever identified them? Is this whole Sunday church thing just about being politically correct?"

Whenever we examine these matters of doctrine, it is never a matter of *who* is right, but rather of *what* is right. Egos and personalities are nonexistent. In any quest for truth, the definitive question should be: "Is it Scriptural?"

The undeniable results of faith in action are frequently perceived to be missing in our churches. These powerful manifestations are the very hallmark of that which we call authentic Christianity.

We need to be introduced to the concept, and challenge of authentic Christianity. This calls for the direct application of the principles that Jesus' taught us in His parables. Spirituality is not a Sunday duty. *It is the power of the Holy Spirit daily working through man to achieve the will of God.*

Sharply focussed, authentic Christianity separates the synthetic from the authentic. Were this done, it would be as dramatic as the raising of the dead. Christ's teachings in action would equate with an 8.9 magnitude earthquake on the "Christian-Richter" scale!

Scattered among these writings are comments made by Steven. They show up unexpectedly—just as they occurred. We are close friends and wilderness dwellers. We are also kayakers, and wildlife videographers. On some of our more wild expeditions, I ran a lot of the *Wiser-Mouse Legacy* by him. He is very tolerant. I sometimes tease Steven about his over-use of the word "like", which is common to most of his age group! However, Steven's unique talents lie in the way in which he can change any inhospitable wilderness day into a happy experience. Almost like magic, he creates a roaring fire, and red-hot, sweet, or "spiked" coffee quickly appears. At supper time his "Bambi-stew" with onions is hard to beat!

In the face of a predatory Black or Grizzly encounter— Steven calmly handles his rifle like a fluid extension of himself. It is an effortless reflex reaction that I admire. It is also an ability I may never acquire. He is also ultimately tuned to wilderness danger-frequencies. Often he observes or senses the approach of bears before my awareness kicks-in. Maybe it's just that I'm too engrossed in text—but Steven is a loyal and competent companion—regardless of the adventure.

Focussing on reality and truth, we need to note that the simple teachings of our Lord Jesus Christ have to be activated. We may have many wonderful software programs on our computers, but they are useless until they are activated. Note that activation needs contact with the software creator. It is the same with us. Christian spiritual activation needs contact with our Creator!

Such were my thoughts as I rambled through the forest surrounding our retreat. In self-examination, I realized that in debate, I usually yielded to those with deeper learning and theological training. This created a sense of being inadequate, and tended to erode my self-esteem. The truth is, that many Christians do feel like nobodies. In reality, we are the sons of God!

It is written: "You did not choose Me, but I chose you and appointed you that you should go and bear fruit." (John 15:16).

People in various church assemblies have asked me: "Derek, when and where did you come to the Lord?" I have to explain that it was no Fourth of July fireworks type of event. As a child with no spiritual upbringing, or church attendance; I had an intense desire based on what I had heard, to become a missionary.

I thought and spoke as a child of innocence. As an adult with little spiritual guidance, and only occasional forays into the Bible; my quest for truth and meaning went deeply into the metaphysical area. Unwittingly, I became enamoured of the cults that recognized God, but denied the sovereignty of our Lord Jesus Christ.

Many years later, full of enthusiasm over another new cult book I'd just read, I dropped into a local tire shop to see my good friend Kerry. Almost immediately, I drowned him in the "real" truth, and handed him the book. He declined to reach for it. Instead, he picked up his Bible off the front desk, and turning to me said: "Derek, when was the last time you read *this* book?"

"Oh that!" I exclaimed, "I know all about that!" Kerry gifted me a look which stopped me cold. It shut me down completely. I listened, and from then on I studied the Holy Scriptures. For me, this was the definitive pivotal-shift point from the cults to Christianity. I learned about the spirit of truth, and the spirit of error.

Eventually, one icy December morning I was baptized in the Nimpkish River on North Vancouver Island. This launched my Christian quest for spiritual wisdom, and Christian maturity. I had begun my journey to become a son of God. It has culminated in *The Wiser-Mouse Legacy!*

Our retreat, like many other good things, came to an end. As always, following such enriching interaction with fellow Christians, numerous questions arose. Some of them gave rise to problems and dilemmas that for me could only be dealt with in earthly solitude.

Ventures of this type call for getting lost on an off shore remote island location. Certainly, some place far from the haunts of man. A place for a walkabout, for several weeks if need be. One needs to be alone with oneself, and the Holy Spirit.

In these wild expeditions, a tendency to merge with all creation takes dominance. On this occasion I had seen *my* sea otters just off shore; and in the evening, my own retreat became my living Eden. I called to the sandpipers, and, nostrils flexed, scented the gentle wash of waves on the sand below.

I gazed with awe into the heavens, brilliant with the lights from an infinite number of worlds. "Our Father is the Father of lights," I murmured. Countless were the number of starlit nights that I had thusly stood in similar rapture, gazing into the night skies. "In my Father's house are many mansions", I quoted.

Warm and secure in my sleeping bag, I was content. To complete this starlit ecstasy, my whole inner being embraced new heights of oneness with our heavenly Father. I *became* the starlit night, and rode the lilting cries of the shore birds.

Softly, I floated with them into the twilight vistas of dream. A seal barked lonely greetings to the rising moon from across the bay. The night was orchestrated by the rhythmic lap of waves, as they kissed time before passing into eternity. Only the eternal "now" remained.

When the reality of the next day dawned; I recollected the Christian retreat, and decided that some type of action was necessary, starting with me! Just what did I believe?

I had been questioning others, almost as though I were an all knowing super pastor; with all the answers, plus a few miracles thrown in for good measure! Of course this is not so. I am merely a "Christian in growth" attempting to identify reality as I see it.

I am driven to locate where I *am*, in relation to what *is* and what should *be*, according to the scriptures. Had I, any more than those I questioned, been able to show works through my faith? Once more I focussed on authentic Christianity, where we fully embrace the spiritual truth that: "Nothing originates with us, everything comes from God."

Some of the concepts we explore may cause the reader to experience a shift in mode or habit of thinking. This would equate to thinking "outside of the box". Old beliefs may need to be restructured as the status quo is dethroned!

To adapt to change is difficult. We must consistently set aside old concepts and embrace new ones. As we learn, we are daily unlearning something that has cost us a lot of effort to acquire in the first place.

Certain anomalies will be discovered in our spiritual explorations that challenge established boundaries of thought. Dare we risk opening our internal ears and eyes to other realities? Jonathan Swift reminds us that: *"Vision is the art of seeing things invisible."*

In yielding to grace, and the indwelling Holy Spirit, new vistas opened for me in this writing; as may also be the case for the reader. To develop power to move mountains through *"Now-Faith";* and to link the concepts of "time" and "eternity" into daily life, are both inspiring and rewarding.

There is nothing dramatically new in these spiritual insights, except perhaps in the manner in which these tinted words of inspiration are painted. The real earth and heaven shaking events that may take place will have to be experienced. Great moments of insight bring about exhilarating forms of spiritual growth.

Not so long ago, a pastor asked me: "Derek, why are you a Christian?" It was a simple question that called for a brief, succinct reply, regardless of its source. Judging by my ineffectual response, I discovered that it behoves we Christians to be scripturally prepared and to quickly respond to such queries; for of such, is the kingdom of God.

A wide, deep chasm separates the speculative thoughts and writings of *natural-man*, from that of the live, spiritual experiences of the *awakened-man*. Whereas the former is surreal; the latter speaks from the attained reality of the selfless, higher, timeless dimension that approaches the state of "I AM".

This treatise is really a "Manual of Operation" for our flight-path to eternity. The entire cosmos is eternally in motion. The galaxies, the stars, the planets in their circuits, and the whole of humanity are immersed in passing time. We are speeding to the end of our physical lives on earth.

Our state of being is a mere parenthesis in this eternity. It discovers most of us dwelling in a dream world that we mistake for reality. It is time to fully awaken.

At commencement of this writing, the main objective was to clearly identify my own spiritual beliefs, and to define the doctrine of authentic Christianity with which I so passionately identify. It was intended for *my* satisfaction only. However, with the additional wisdom of *Wiser-Mouse*, this whole book took on a spiritual life of its own, whereby I merely created the record!

This little volume as a spiritual manual for our flight-path to eternity. It is a record of *Time-man* graduating into the spiritual state of *Now-Man*, indwelt by the Holy Spirit, preparing for ascension. It is a "how to" guide, to actually living faith-driven authentic Christianity.

CHAPTER TWO

We know that man as he is, soul and body only, is incomplete. A whole man is a tripartite being. He is spirit, soul, and body. This is not a given. It is up to free-will man to determine his own course. He will either develop himself into a complete being, or he will not. This task of completion has to be effected by him in this lifetime. It will fully equip him for the next stage of his odyssey. It is required of man to launch his ascension as a spiritual being.

Each of us will make our own decisions in this matter. We may have foggy concepts of the world to come, or some other idea of afterlife. These are usually quickly dismissed, and tossed into the maelstrom of daily activity. However, in our quieter moments of contemplation of this earthly existence as incomplete man, we may not be able to ignore the messages from within. Were we to do so, it would be at our peril. These internal communications may disturb our equilibrium. However, we need to cultivate the habit of listening, receiving, and giving them our full consideration. That is their purpose.

The *Wiser-Mouse Legacy* is a personal flight manual of Instruction. It is for those who wish to enter the realms of eternity after we cease to exist on Earth. We have limited time to prepare for takeoff, and it behoves us to take action now. All we ever have had, or ever will have, is the eternal *now.*

This is more than just a shop-manual to study how we should live our lives here on planet Earth. It contains in-depth instructions on how to attain some very sophisticated internal awareness.

We arrive here on Earth fully equipped with all the basics required for our flight into eternity. Those of us who have glimpsed the vision of eternal life will be seeking guidance. Our sojourn here is so brief, that time is of the absolute essence.

For that reason alone, we should be diligently seeking *meaning* that is empowered by *purpose* and *direction*. It will take time to study and to adopt the stress-free lifestyle they offer. It may entail a steep learning curve. However, it is a reality we richly deserve.

Wilderness explorer-friend Steven, whom we have already introduced, fully understands the meaning of the biblical term "long suffering". He has been subjected to so much oratory in the reading aloud of *The Wiser-Mouse Legacy*; that at times he has demanded, "Time-out!"

We will have to be *awake* to accomplish our objectives. We have been born into a world that is not exactly what it appears to be. It is comprised mostly of solid, live or apparently dead substances. Only about 10 percent of this reality is experienced, and that through our five bodily senses.

We have to recognize that about 90 percent of life and living encompasses an invisible world. We are immersed in this unseen dimension. We may not care to acknowledge this fact, but it does comprise a major part of our spiritual lives. "For in Him we live and move and have our being." (Acts 17:28).

We need to invest an adequate amount of time in the study of our operations manual, the Holy Bible. If we do not seriously commit ourselves to this spiritual learning process, we cannot reasonably expect to achieve a successful takeoff at graduation, our time of passing.

By then, we should consciously be in the full power of faith in our heavenly Father. It is imperative that we demand of ourselves a committed view of Christianity and of God. Is He to us some kind of indifferent authority to be regarded with respect from a great distance? Is He sort of "up there someplace"? Or do we have a close, ongoing spiritual relationship with Him?

Whether we like it or not, we are required to leave our bodies sometime due to old age, disease, or perhaps sudden mishap. It is high time that we recognized that the intimate *I* within each of us is something apart from our bodies. Each of us has a body, but *I* am not my body.

It is written in 1 Corinthians 13:3: "And though I bestow all my goods to feed *the poor*, and though I give my body to be burned, and have not love, it profits me nothing." This does not refer to the body alone; it says, "and though *I* give my body," referring to an entity apart from the body. Although this is quite simplistic, it is not generally recognized.

Our Holy Bible reveals that we are spirit, soul, and body. We live in this temple (body) of the Holy Spirit. Herein resides the power of one's immortal self. Christians speak of being indwelt by the Holy Spirit, and in doing so they refer to having emptied themselves of "self". They now acknowledge and rely on the guidance of the Holy Spirit.

This has nothing to do with theory or logic. It is an addition to logic, and too few of us actually attain this indwelt state. It requires us to permit the Holy Spirit to move in and through us. God is Spirit, as are we, and this is a spiritual journey.

"Truth lived is Godly empowerment. The Holy Scriptures are Man's ultimate guide. When Man has experienced messages from God through the Holy Spirit, and has lived them in obedience, it is a record of spiritual reality that can never be forgotten or denied." (From the Lost Notebooks of Wiser-Mouse).

Many Christians express their disappointment in their own spiritual growth; whereby they may live the Christian life of abundance as Christ taught. Despite their best efforts, they feel trapped in a cul-de-sac of frustration, even though their church is supportive.

When scriptural truth is observed to be in conflict with the practices of institutionalized religion, it slowly drains individual commitment. The Christian unwittingly retreats into his own "habitual church trance". Spiritual progress is negated.

How sad it is that we go through the motions of Christianity like dancers in a shadowy dream. It is high time that we stopped the dance of illusion, and turned the lights up high! It is time to drop the varied masks of disbelief and to devote our spiritual efforts to facing up to reality. How much longer will we persist in, "having a form of godliness but denying its power?" (2 Timothy 3:5).

Many churches are seeking an increase in membership as they believe they have much to offer. Perhaps that is true, but when asked how they will accomplish this, it is explained that they will "pray for the increase." They believe their trust and faith in God will provide results in due time. It would appear from this viewpoint that no one is actively involved with the church's strategic and tactical planning, if indeed such planning exists. Knowing looks are observed, along with benign smiles of impotence that forecast nothing is going to change.

The reality is that any desired expansion has to start with us. Man has to act firstly in faith, without purse or scrip if necessary. Waiting for the Holy Spirit to act while we stand by in prayer, is the same as a farmer expecting his land to be magically tilled, whereupon he will give God a helping hand.

Let us imagine an industrious salesperson, *not* making prospective calls and contacts to show his offering. Instead, he stays in his hotel and prays for the increase. (It ain't gonna happen). We need to act first in faith.

Throughout our journey, we will always have a great deal more to learn about Christianity. In general, it presents itself to us through a wide range of denominations, cults, and beliefs. In our everyday lives, we have too little time to devote to the evaluation of these numerous beliefs and practices. Were we to do so; the purpose would be to compare and determine if our current church connections are *authentic*. That is, are they foundationally based on adherence to the Holy Bible? Only from this will we recognize true spirituality.

In regard to our shortage of time, just for fun, check out 2 Peter 3:8: "But, beloved, do not forget this one thing, that with the Lord one day *is* as a thousand years, and a thousand years as one day." This scale shows us, to some small degree, where we are in the cosmic scene.

Let us briefly come to grips with some timely facts! If 1000 years is one day, 500 years is 12 hours, 250 years is 6 hours, 125 years is 3 hours, and 62.5 years is only 1.5 hours! No wonder we never seem to get things done! We live only for about an hour and a half on the cosmic time scale!

It would also appear that: "The Lord is not slack concerning *His* promise, as some count slackness." (2 Peter 3:9). He has only been away for a couple of days, based on His time!

We need to examine what type of Christian doctrine or belief system we now hold. This is of paramount importance. We should ask ourselves if we have a clear understanding of what it comprises.

Is that which is currently practiced in our Christian assembly scripturally sound? Are the "roles" of the Trinity clearly defined? We need to recognize that we are spirits dwelling within bodies. This is an all-important element in our spiritual understanding.

"While we do not look at the things which are seen, but at things which are not seen. For the things which are seen *are* temporary, but the things which are not seen *are* eternal. (2 Corinthians 4:18).

Note that the physical, *natural-man,* cannot comprehend the *spiritual-man*. Spiritual truths are above and beyond logical reasoning, and therefore cannot be explained intellectually. An authentic Christian is he who is indwelt by Jesus Christ. Christians recognize His sovereignty and obey His teachings.

Many people consider themselves "Christian", simply because they go to church, or because they live in a Christian nation. But simply going to church, doing a lot of work for charities, and being a moral and upright citizen does not make us Christians; any more than going into a car dealership turns us into a car.

The Bible alerts us in Titus 3:5: "Not by works of righteousness which we have done, but according to His mercy He saved us, through the washing of regeneration and renewing of the Holy Spirit". That should give us pause for consideration.

We Christians need to experience our Lord Jesus Christ as man and God. We need to understand what Jesus meant when He said: "And then I will declare to them, I never knew you; depart from Me, you who practice lawlessness!" (Matthew 7:23). We also need to pay attention to Jesus' statement: "Assuredly, I say to you, I do not know you". (Matthew 25:12).

It is not just a matter of whether we know Jesus. Based on His "I do not know you" statement, it is also a matter of whether Jesus knows us. Our explorations into our man-God relationship with Jesus will slowly unfold within our text.

More importantly, we need to monitor our spiritual growth and identify just where we really stand between our triune God and ourselves. We raise one soul-searching question early. Are we pseudo-Christians, or are we authentic Christians? We need to make a definite choice. It is a life and death affair. "Pseudo" is defined as being spurious or sham.

A writer from the 16th century said: "The modern Christians have buildings of stone, wherein they serve the goddess of vanity. They congregate where they may exhibit their fine clothes and the preacher his learning."

Do we recognize any similarity between then and now? Have we changed *that* much from the sixteenth to the twenty-first century? We suggest not!

In these days, masses of professing Christians are totally ignorant of, or indifferent to, biblical truths. Many churches today are places where Christians gather on Sundays to feel comfortable, and to gain reassurance of their beliefs through formalism, and dead rituals. People accept that which "is", in all innocence. Spiritual hunger may or may not eventually gnaw at them.

But, they do not override their church programming, nor do they shed tears. They just relapse into church-like compliance. "My people are destroyed for lack of knowledge." (Hosea 4:6).

Individually, we Christians of today need to take stock, and rid ourselves of habitual attitudes of "hopeful niceness", which is a cover-up for "passive defeat".

Are we missing the mark? We need to get on track! No progress can be made without specific plans to change ourselves, and our assemblies. If we do not act, we may as well be among the ranks of the "living dead". (Not a rock band!).

As we examine this scenario, we are immediately confronted with a dilemma. It is this; we consistently fail to differentiate between "symptoms" and "problems". There is a need to be definitive in our understanding of these terms, or, we will react by treating a *symptom* as a *problem*. We need to accurately diagnose a situation, before formulating action-plans and objectives.

Symptoms, when finally identified, are subjective evidence of collective happenings that are disturbing, way out of order, imbalanced, or cause for concern.

Problems, are usually packaged groups of symptoms often unrelated to one another. They are usually a source of perplexity, distress or vexation, and they may involve intricate unsettling questions.

If these factors are correctly defined, endeavours to introduce change in individuals, as well as assemblies, may be successful. We need to stand back to get perspective. In our Christian growth and learning curve, we need to accept that it is *our* responsibility to achieve our own spiritual progress; *not* entirely that of the pastor. (For reference, throughout our text, we refer to pastors as *him*. This is an inclusive gender term).

"Natural Man dwells in a spiritual void. He is a living entity of symptoms that proclaim this state. He is both alive, and dead, in time, and the world of illusion. The solution to his problem is in his spiritual awakening. Then only, can he be a complete human being." (From the Lost Notebooks of Wiser-Mouse).

We are 100 percent accountable to our Lord Jesus Christ in the matter of spiritual development. This duty rests squarely on our shoulders.

We speak of *accountability*, which in turn is linked to *responsibility*, and to *authority*. All three are interrelated. Let us quickly confirm what they mean!

Responsibility is the duty assigned to a position, in our case as a *son of God*. It always originates from a superior-subordinate relationship. It is a form of continuing obligation and cannot be delegated. Those who have accepted responsibility are fully accountable to a higher power for their performance.

Accountability is the liability created for use of authority, in the Christian's case, God. It is the answerability for a standard of performance. Our immediate supervisor is the Holy Spirit.

Authority is the power to exact obedience. Authority is the principle at the root of organization, requiring action from others. In Christianity, there is no power of authority higher than that of God.

These are good definitions to superimpose on our thinking, for they are all directly related to obedience; a subject that we shall explore later.

One Christian matter that needs early clarification is the matter of baptism; as it relates to babies, infants and adults. It can be the subject of debate, and involve much disagreement. The baptism of babies is not located in the Holy Scriptures. We also need to separate the term "babies", from "infants", although, in our text we treat them as one and the same.

It would appear however, that baptism of babies follow only the traditions and wordy validations of men. The premise is: that "baby-baptism" ensures that he receives forgiveness of sins, is redeemed from death, and receives eternal salvation, right from the moment of conception.

The child, whether exposed to the ceremony of christening or baptism, is totally unconscious of what has transpired, [although this is argued as otherwise]. Later, as teens, these young Christians are processed through classes to receive their "confirmation". This is performed to confirm their previous; "in-the-womb", full knowledge and understanding of their spiritual status, including salvation and commitment to Christ.

The terms "christening" and "baptism", are often used interchangeably, even though they are different. By christening a child, the parents make a promise to raise him in a Christian life-style. In this rite, the child is sprinkled with water. Some denominations refer to infant christening as baptism. The well-meaning people who practice christening or infant baptism, often believe the ceremony has "something to do" with the salvation of the child.

In authentic Christian baptism, the individual is "of age", and is conscious of that which he is undertaking. This baptismal rite is performed as full water immersion. It is a *covenant of inviolate conscious commitment between man and God.*

Baptism publicly declares that one has fully repented, [experienced a change of mind], and accepted Jesus Christ as his Saviour. Man is "born again", this time, in the Spirit. By this act, man commits to Jesus' sacrifice on the cross, His sovereignty, and His teachings.

If the distinctions between christening and baptism were not clearly understood; later, as a committed adult Christian, it would be frightening to discover that one had been processed through these rites, and not received salvation. Immutably, true salvation is a matter of mature cognizance.

It will be seen that personal salvation is different. It is recognition that we are sinners, [doing other than the will of God], and are willing to turn away from sin [repent]. It is in believing that Jesus Christ died for us, was buried, and rose from the dead. Through prayer, we invite Jesus into our lives as our personal Saviour.

The doctrine in this text recognizes only the Christian water-immersion baptism.

"When Man in the Spirit 'comes to himself', his yearning for the Presence of God will be publicly consummated in his Holy Baptism. He will become one with the Body of Christ." (From the Lost Notebooks of Wiser-Mouse).

Basically there are two groups of people in the world today, those who believe on the Son, and those who do not. The

Word of God never simply says believe and be saved, but rather, believe on the Lord Jesus Christ and be saved. "For God so loved the world that He gave His only begotten Son, that whosoever believes in Him should not perish but have everlasting life." (John 3:16).

It is not enough just to believe; a person must believe in Him. When the Philippian jailer asked: "Sirs, what must I do to be saved?" Paul and Silas said, "Believe on the Lord Jesus Christ, and you will be saved, you and your household." (Acts 16:30-31).

We may, or may not, be associated with an assembly that is practicing *scriptural* Christianity. Although Christian church assemblies meet regularly for worship services and fellowship; they are usually unaware of their *church doctrine*, or of their personal level of Christian comprehension. Despite this, we may be assured that our Lord Jesus Christ will meet any one of us, exactly at our level of Christian understanding at any time.

Our congregations are always comprised of individuals at different levels of spiritual attainment.

Firstly, there are the un-churched new members who have come to the assembly to see what it is all about. These could be described as *seeker* Christians.

Secondly, there are those who are in a static state where awakening or re-awakening has to occur. Dare we label these the *static* Christians? They would include the *baby Christians,* who are still drinking the *milk* of the word even after many years. They are content with the traditional status quo. This category also includes those who just "do church" on Sunday.

Thirdly, there are those who are leaning toward maturity, but may have reached a plateau. Some are just marking time and gaining insight before continuing their Christian journey. These may be the *plateau* Christians. They are consciously applying Christian faith principles in their lives with powerful results. However, they, like all of us, still have a very long way to go.

Finally, there are the *mature* Christians who are still growing in their Christ-like attributes. They dwell with ever greater frequency in the Presence of God.

These are they of the engrafted Word; who have achieved an intimate awareness and communication with God through our Lord Jesus Christ. Their lives are primarily directed by the Holy Spirit. Truly, they are examples of "Thy will be done."

For a Christian to stay on track, he will need to have fully accepted the Bible as his infallible resource on all spiritual matters. "fully accepted", means that we do not partially accept this, or partially reject that!

It is vital for those of the engrafted word, to recognize and embrace the entire Bible as an agreement. It is a covenant between man and God. Regardless of where any of we Christians are in our continued learning, we've all had problems with reading and comprehending the Scriptures.

It's the same for any one of us when a friend recommends a book from which he received great insight. When we read it, or try to, we discover that we are not on the same wavelength. Then, a year or two later, we pick up that same book, and Bingo! It all makes sense, but only because our internal state finally became receptive to it.

Some Christians ruefully exclaim, as I have at times: "When did they add that to the Bible?" It is a common experience to see or understand a passage differently, even after having read it so many times before!

The Bible is comprised of sixty-six books. It was written by about forty different authors over a period of some fifteen hundred years. These writers came from all walks of life.

They were kings, fishermen, priests, government officials, farmers, shepherds, and doctors with vastly different educational backgrounds. They also came from many different cultures, three continents, and three different languages.

But that which places the Bible above anything that could be possibly written by mere man; is that it contains such remarkable diversity, with such incredible unity. Hundreds of subjects are covered, not just one, yet the Bible retains its unity.

There is complete harmony which cannot be explained by coincidence or collusion. The Bible was written under divine inspiration. There are common themes throughout, and Jesus is the central character. The whole book is really about Him.

The Old Testament prophecy is about Jesus' entrance into the world. The New Testament describes His coming, and His work to bring salvation to our sinful world. A testament is a covenant, a written agreement or promise between two people or parties; in this case between God and man.

Let us remember, that had it not been for a host of God-inspired Protestants, we would still be denied access to the Holy Scriptures. Thousands of dedicated Christians indwelt by the Holy Spirit have sacrificed their lives in order for us to possess Bibles. Were it not for them, we may now be totally under the rule of satanic powers through man-made religions.

The Bible brings most readers to the limits of their understanding very quickly. It is not a book of logic. It is a book of pure spiritual wisdom. Nor can any man-made religion plumb the depths of the Bible by endeavouring to reduce it to plain human logic.

The Holy Bible is not a book of *esotericism*; of that which is *esoteric.* So what is esotericism? It signifies the holding of esoteric opinions or beliefs, that is, ideas preserved or understood by a small group of those specially initiated. It pertains to that which is more inward and mystic. The antonym of "esoteric", [meaning opposite], is "exoteric". The Holy Bible is definitively exoteric [opposite] to esotericism.

It is not our intent to write a theological treatise on this matter. Suffice it to simply say, that the following words are identified, and associated with the esoteric.

To mention but a few: The Occult, Numerology, Scientology, Mysticism, Divination, Freemasonry, Karma, Cosmic Consciousness, Esoteric Christianity, Reincarnation, Theosophy by Madam Blavatsky, and those involved with Spiritualism and Astrology. The list goes on with various sub-divisions of beliefs.

Our Lord Jesus Christ gave us quite distinctive interpretations of physical *natural-man,* versus the awakened *spiritual-man*. Through parables, He strove to open the consciousness of man to that which lies beyond the five senses; that is, being born again in the Spirit through Christ.

Christianity is a state of committed spirituality. Until a person recognizes that his own wisdom and intelligence are not sufficient, he cannot be receptive to God's greater wisdom.

Inasmuch that the Bible brings us to what is known as "religion"; we need to define our interpretation of religion. This term is usually employed as a catch-all phrase for all matters pertaining to God and man. (Webster says it is: "A personal set or institutionalized system of religious attitudes or beliefs or practices.")

Generally, all of Christianity operates under the "umbrella" term of "religion". Churches are denominational, as in Baptist, Catholic, Anglican, Lutheran, United, et cetera. In our treatise, we recognize that "authentic" Christianity is non-denominational. Authenticity is based on strict adherence to the Holy Scriptures. No tradition, formalism, or religious crutches are employed.

Authentic Christian churches are a part of the living Body of Christ. Whether it is of two or more gathered in My Name, or an entire church assembly, *the church is a living, growing organism*. It is not an organization within a building structure. Authentic Christians live in harmony, and obedience to the individual roles of the Godhead, according to the Holy Scriptures.

All regular churches purportedly comprise the "Body of Christ". However, churches and beliefs are so divided, that one's choice may well be based on blind trust and lack of knowledge. One's particular church affiliation is a critical decision, the fruit of which is either eternal life or death.

Most denominational churches are steeped in tradition, and practice what is known as institutionalized religion. They work from regular Bibles, and the services are rigid. There is little evidence of the Holy Spirit's Presence, or of Godly commitment.

Some churches are primarily soul-based. Their power lies in statues, crosses, candles, rituals, and liturgies, along with traditional buildings with stained glass windows depicting Christian scenes. There are also richly coloured robes, along with formal procedures. Services have an aura of mystery. This tends to hypnotize people into a form of religious submission which is rarely questioned.

In many church assemblies, the ecclesiastical fraternity control the congregation, and do their thinking on spiritual matters for them. The congregation, [sheep], may be unwittingly grateful that *their* responsibility and accountability to God, is on someone else's shoulders. The sheep are led captive, and yield to the dogma of the church authority. No sheep ever attempt to validate practiced church doctrine with the Holy Scriptures. This is the practise of "surreal" religion. (Webster: "Surreal, having the intense irrational reality of a dream").

Our text will not mediate in the area relating to confession and the forgiveness of sins. It too, is an area that is rife with deviant religious practise. Many Christians are required to go through a priest or pastor to obtain forgiveness on a personal basis, or are forgiven as an entire congregation. These practices are diametrically opposed to the Word of God. To whom or what have these Christians yielded their spiritual responsibility? Have they not read the Word? "For *there* is one God and one Mediator between God and men, *the* Man Christ Jesus." (1 Timothy 2:5).

When we place our trust in any church, pastor, or priest, as mediator between us and God; we have acknowledged that authority as having equality with the Father, the Lord Jesus

Christ, and the Holy Spirit. We need to diligently screen contexts for improprieties versus the Bible.

The doctrine of authentic Christianity is that the sins of man can only be forgiven by the Father, through the Lord Jesus Christ, by those indwelt by the Holy Spirit.

We are simply confirming how hypocrisy is as rampant today, as it was in times of old. We need to be aware of the many religions that are at variance with the true teachings of our Lord Jesus Christ, and how easy it is to be led astray. Jesus vehemently rejected Pharisee-type religions associated with hypocrisy, while He was on Earth.

Authentic Christianity differs from religion. Its churches truly comprise the Body of Christ. Through grace, each individual has an ongoing personal spiritual relationship with our heavenly Father, through our Lord Jesus; and he lives under the guidance of the Holy Spirit.

Some religions view being "born again", and being guided by the Holy Spirit with reticence. It is not of primary focus in their active belief system and practise. Still other religions place significant emphasis on these spiritual elements. Being *born again* is foundational to Christianity.

It is written: "Jesus answered and said to him, [Nicodemus], 'Most assuredly, I say to you, unless one is born again, he cannot enter the kingdom of God.' 4: Nicodemus said to him: 'How can a man be born when he is old? Can he enter a second time into his mother's womb and be born?'" (John 3:3-4).

5: "Jesus answered, 'Most assuredly, I say to you, unless one is born of water and of the Spirit, he cannot enter into the kingdom of God. 6: That which is born of flesh is flesh;

and that which is born of the Spirit is spirit. 7: Do not marvel that I said to you, You must be born again'.'"

Authentic Christianity recognizes the role of the Holy Spirit in relation to the Father: "However, when He, the Spirit of truth, has come, He will guide you into all truth; for He will not speak of His own authority, but whatever He hears He will speak; and He will tell you things to come." (John 16:13).

Christians need to realize the importance of faith in understanding God's word. We come first in humility to our Lord Jesus Christ, and surrender our whole being to His doctrines, commands, and teachings. It is an act of losing ourselves. It is an emptying of self. In this manner we are "born again"; this time in the Spirit. In so doing, we receive our gift of salvation and eternal life.

True Christianity starts with the individual, and is founded on a personal relationship with the members of the Holy Trinity. The individual, indwelt by the Holy Spirit, becomes part of the Body of Christ in an assembly that practices authentic Christianity.

Let us envision an instrument mounted on a tripod supported by three rock-solid legs. The instrument cannot perform to its designed perfection without that stable foundation. So it is with we who are instruments of Christ.

To perform to our designed potential perfection, we too require stability. Let us imagine our triune-selves as tripods for a moment! The three rock-solid legs at our base are the Father, the Lord Jesus Christ, and the Holy Spirit. There is nothing shaky about that! With this foundation; we the instrument, can achieve all that our "operating manual", [the Holy Bible], lays out for our life-styles on Earth.

We now need to further examine the three persons of God in the Godhead. It is a difficult concept to comprehend. We have three personages who act as one. They interact with each other, and each has a definite role in relationship to us.

So how do we comprehend this Trinity? It is called an "antinomy". [Webster: "A contradiction between two equally valid principles or inferences correctly drawn from those principles"]. Gasp! In simple terms, it means "against the law of human reasoning"!

That which is comprehensible to God, maybe quite antinomical to man. What is antinomical to a dog for example, is quite understandable to man. The two most obvious biblical antinomies are the Trinity, and the divine-human nature of Jesus.

We read in Luke 10:21: "In that hour Jesus rejoiced in the Spirit and said, 'I thank You, Father, Lord of heaven and earth, that You have hidden these things from *the* wise and prudent and revealed them to babes'."

We need to recognize that it is only through Jesus Christ that we have access to God, our heavenly Father. It is written: "I am the way, the truth, and the life. No one comes to the Father except through Me." (John 14:6). Note also: "No one can come to Me unless the Father who sent Me draws him; and I will raise him up at the last day." (John 6:44).

It is only through *obedience* to our Lord Jesus Christ that we become truly Christian. All matters pertaining to planet Earth including the final judgement of man, has been placed by the Father in the hands of the Son, our Lord Jesus Christ: "All authority has been given to Me in heaven and on earth." (Matt 28:18).

It is important that we confirm that the Holy Spirit is a personage. He is a person. He is not a quantifiable factor as in a commodity, [like filling something up], but is a personage.

The Holy Spirit is only referred to as "He", never "it". We are indwelt by the Holy Spirit. We can study the forms in which the Holy Spirit appeared, by His actions. His appearances may vary as when he was with the apostles:

"And suddenly there came a sound from heaven as of a rushing mighty wind, and it filled the house where they were sitting. Then there appeared to them divided tongues, as of fire, and *one* sat upon each of them. And they were all filled with the Holy Spirit and began to speak in tongues, as the Spirit gave them utterance." (Acts 2:2-4). In Matthew 3:16 we read: "And He saw the Spirit of God descending like a dove, and alighting upon him."

"Yes Steven?"

"Like ... I'm ... Christian ... like ... but I don't go to no church like. My church ... like ... is all around me in the wilderness ... not like ... in some fancy building like ..."

"Yes Steven, exactly, but your very life depends on with whom you fellowship, and where you go to church."

"I suppose like ... I hope like ... there's people like me there ... like ... it'll take some time."

"The true Christian is indwelt by the Holy Spirit. His church is within his soul. He joins with other Christians whenever and wherever he can. His God-consciousness is unbroken. He is part of the Body of Christ." (From the Lost Notebooks of Wiser-Mouse).

Let us now examine what can be done to further assist our Christian journey, regardless of where we stand in spiritual growth. In doing so, we will need to investigate those described in the Holy Bible as the "living-dead", or the unawakened.

If a man is only able to think psychologically, and has no concept of that which is spiritual, he is only intellectually in contact with his external world. Being glued to his five senses, he will remain an undeveloped man. He needs to change now! In this life! This is a spiritual world.

"Man is beset by feelings of not knowing who he is, or what he is." (From the Lost Notebooks of Wiser-Mouse).

So, where and how, can any of we earnest Christian seekers, be assisted in our odyssey toward maturity? For a start, if we may be so bold, let us state that it would be a great step forward for all of Christianity, were we to adopt commonality in our terminology.

We speak of: Hope, Sin, Forgiveness, Salvation, Belief, Doctrine, Faith, Prayer, Grace, Tithing, Soul, Spirit and Obedience. Regardless of context, it is imperative that we are quite definitive as to what is meant by each of these terms.

Otherwise, we could be like a carpenter's apprentice being taught that he is to hold the head of the hammer, and hit the nail with the handle. In Christian practise and Bible studies, it is not uncommon to discover that devoted Christians are way off base in correctly understanding many of these quite critical words.

Christian terms and words are the very well-springs of spiritual life, but they are still only concepts. One must go through the experiences of the words in order to believe them. We can live in fear, pain and need, or follow the teachings of Christ. It's our choice!

Further, let us recognize that we tend to gloss over these matters far too lightly. In discussions among Christians, these questions are often seen as inconsequential, or brushed off as a matter of semantics. Can one *bend* the Scriptures to meet with one's own understanding? It is written: "Knowing this first, that no prophesy of Scripture is of any private interpretation." (2 Peter 1:20). Additionally: "The Scripture cannot be broken." (John 10:35).

If we fail to come up with accurate interpretations, let us together research such matters under the authority of the Bible. This is another hallmark of authentic Christianity. Note its lack of ego involvement. It is a humble and level approach on the playing field of ignorance that allows all parties to grow spiritually.

Let us be careful! That word semantics is not a license that allows us to side-slip an important question. We either know or we do not. *Semantics*, being a study of meanings, is closely related to the word interpret.

We cannot take these matters too lightly. In analyzing these concepts we must recognize that there is nothing new under the sun. The words employed here have been around for over two thousand years.

This is also a matter of accountability in effective teaching and learning. We must assist our pastors by making our needs known to them. It is easy to find fault with teaching. We have the responsibility of asking questions of our pastors on those Christian matters which we may not understand. We need to arrange an appointment for a specified period of time to achieve this. It cannot be handled within an after service fellowship meeting, or in a matter of two minutes over a coffee! We need privacy too.

Two key questions need to be addressed. What is authentic Christianity? And what is an authentic Christian?

"The practise of authentic Christianity is that of Man consciously applying the spiritual principles that Christ taught. It is grace-gifted empowerment that unleashes the authority and power of God." (From the Lost Notebooks of Wiser-Mouse).

An authentic Christian must be quite sure of what he believes, and why. His actions must portray that Christianity is founded not just on the teachings of Jesus, but on Who He is.

The sovereignty of our Lord Jesus Christ is at the apex of this concept; otherwise Christianity is relegated just to the great teachings of Christ only. Therein lays the danger of Jesus being seen as just another prophet. Our Lord Jesus Christ is the Son of God. He was sent to us by our Heavenly Father.

The authentic Christian develops habitual spiritual skills in the live application of the principles that Christ taught. *He brings life to Christianity! He brings Christianity to life!*

An authentic Christian may be seen as a type of radical in comparison to the normal person of most congregations. He may ask questions of the church assembly which they apparently are unable to answer with any conviction. In reality, most Christians are simply ill-equipped to correctly handle the doctrinal questions that should be raised in our churches.

The church that practices authentic Christianity leaves no room for doubt or half measures. Jesus said that if his followers were tepid or lukewarm, He would spew them out of His mouth. [Either you are with Me, or you are against Me]. This applies to all Christians. So let us decide right now. Are we true ambassadors for Christ? We need to get with it! Our God is the God of the living, both here, and in the hereafter.

However, this does not necessarily relegate the rest of Christians to the spiritual scrapheap! When we examine authenticity, we may be able to discern the differences between what genuine Christianity *is*, and that which is *dogma* created by man.

(Dogma is a body of doctrine concerning faith and morals formally stated and authoritatively proclaimed by a church, often without adequate grounds).

In other words, there may be a wide margin of difference between what is practiced in our churches, and that which is biblically correct. Based on this, we may lack genuine understanding of Christ's teachings, or how to live them. The prevailing question which confronts us is:

"If the Christian teaching and practise in our churches is so right, what makes Christians of today so ineffective, so impotent, and so utterly powerless in the face of all the spiritual principles that Jesus taught?"

This is the challenge we face! Where are we? It behoves us to search ourselves with all due diligence under the guidance of the Holy Spirit. Something is wrong somewhere. Again we ask: "What is missing? Is it the lack of authenticity and spiritual commitment?"

Ray Stedman, in his most excellent work entitled *Authentic Christianity*, described five unmistakable marks of an authentic Christian. They are: "Unquenchable optimism, unvarying success, unforgettable impact, unimpeachable integrity and undeniable reality".

We recognize and fully embrace these attributes in the authentic Christian. It is not just *being* a Christian that produces these but *living* as a Christian too.

Other identifying characteristics of an authentic Christian are; that he does not associate with the manufacturers, wholesalers and retailers of man-made religions, traditions or cults.

He is a non-conformist. He lives and acts as a Christian who is in full obedience to the spiritual fact that, all things in heaven and earth originate with God, not man.

His sufficiency is from God. Jesus: "I am the vine, you are the branches. He who abides in Me, and I in him, bears much fruit; for without Me you can do nothing." (John 15:5).

He has accepted the Holy Bible as his ultimate spiritual authority, and adheres to the doctrines of the Holy Scriptures. He walks by faith, and not by sight. In prayer requests, worship, and in giving thanks, he speaks *with* God, not just *to* God.

An authentic Christian walks under the guidance of the Holy Spirit. He is not governed by man in the matter of spiritual wisdom. *He is ordained by God, not by man or church.* He is an ambassador for Christ and the kingdom of heaven. In that capacity he is fully responsible and accountable to our Lord Jesus Christ.

Authentic Christians know that death and life are in the power of the tongue; the spoken word. We need to understand that negativity, illness, loss, as well as financial and physical deprivation, are the "fruits" of the tongue, as are spiritual, mental and bodily health. A distinguishing mark of spiritual maturity in the authentic Christian is his skill, accuracy, and knowledge of God's Word.

Authentic Christians frequently sin [do other than the will of God]. They are still human, the *natural-man*, and subject to error. However they possess sin awareness. They ask God for forgiveness in the name of Jesus. Having received forgiveness, they *fully* accept this gift of grace by *not* retaining *any* element of sin. Sin is like cloud cover. It blocks communication with God in the same manner that rain clouds obscure the sun.

Authentic Christians are actively receptive to intuitive thinking and messages from the Holy Spirit. He will guide them in all truth on their journey of obedience toward perfection in Christ. In the event that a Christian should take offence in discussing matters of doctrine; it may reveal that he still has too strong an element of ego and self-importance.

This would indicate that the "*I*" of "*me*" has not as yet fully yielded to governance of the Holy Spirit. A hallmark of Christian maturity is the emptying of self, and the infilling of the Holy Spirit.

This enables the vacuum to be filled with the Word. In obeying the Holy Spirit, we will discover there are times when we need to embrace obedience, and shelve logic. Obedience is the operative word.

You will recall that just before Jesus left, He said: "But the Helper, the Holy Spirit, whom the Father will send you in My name, He will teach you all things, and bring to your remembrance all things I said to you." (John 14:26).

We learn from Romans 10:17 that faith comes by hearing, and hearing by the word of God. We need to act on the word of James: "But be doers of the word, and not hearers only, deceiving yourselves." (James 1:22).

We need to link obedience with authority, and to master our understanding of authority. God upholds all things by the word of His power. Satan is not afraid of our preaching the Word of Christ, but he is definitely in fear of being subject to the authority of Christ.

"God's throne is established on authority. It is synonymous with active Faith. Man in the Spirit is the highest active expression of God's will." (From the Lost Notebooks of Wiser-Mouse).

Indeed, it is time for renewed vision, and for us to embrace authentic Christianity. Throughout our long Christian journey we will be confronted with disorienting situations both physically and psychologically. We need to be equipped to manage them effectively.

The major key to our spiritual growth is to live by the engrafted Word of God. This means reading, studying and absorbing the Holy Scriptures. If we fail to do this, it is the equivalent of being lost, of having no foundation. Patience! It can be done!

As we proceed, disturbing "objective judgements" may be incurred. We will be examining ourselves and others in matters of belief. The state of our growth toward Christian maturity will come under scrutiny.

Regardless, we may rest assured that Jesus will meet any one of us at any point in our journey. It matters not what our perception of ourselves may be. Jesus already knows each of us as individuals. He is truth and grace in motion.

Let us bring one critical fact into sharp focus. It is this. We never cease to plant thoughts, words and actions. We will always reap the results of those same thoughts, words and deeds. Our whole lives are involved in the process of planting and harvesting every waking hour of each day. *Thusly we create our own realities.*

We need to superimpose mental monitoring or scanning of what we are planting and harvesting. Initially, this will be a conscious act of thinking. Later, after a lot of trial and error, forgetfulness, and lack of self-control, it will become an automatic mode of thinking. It should be habitual. In the world of plants for example, if we want carrots, we sow carrot seeds, not onion seeds. If we want oak trees we plant acorns, not the seeds from pine cones!

"Do not be deceived, God is not mocked; for whatever a man sows, that he will also reap." (Galatians 6:7). The result of what we have been sowing is the fruit of our lives up until this moment in time. We are products of our total thought processes to date. What do we see?

"Wow! Steven! No matter where I stand around our fire the smoke chokes me and blinds me! Is there a message I'm missing?"

"Hey! We planted a fire ... like ... 'an now we's like—reapin' hot coffee ... pass your mug!"

"Thanks Steven! Ooooh! I feel the chills departing!"

Individually, we Christians need to consider our spiritual objectives. We need to become focussed on specific areas of development in our spiritual growth. When these factors have been identified, we can formulate them into personal objectives to be achieved.

If we have no plan for our spiritual growth, we are like milk cows coming into the barn to our stalls at an appointed time to be serviced. Everything is nice; the "hay" is good, and so what? We repeat the cycle endlessly until departure-time, unless we awaken.

To reiterate, we are the sum total of our planting and reaping at any given time. So let us look at ourselves inside and out. Where are we now? We unwittingly designed it! We are accountable for it! We created it! No one else is to blame. We don't like what we see or what we have become? Hold on! All is not lost!

When we come to our Lord Jesus, He forgives and accepts us no matter where we are in life. We may have come from a grossly dysfunctional life-style, toxic family history, or whatever. He will release us from any evil, [darkness] that may hold us in bondage.

Jesus said: "Come to Me, all *you* who labor and are heavy laden, and I will give you rest. Take My yoke upon you and learn from Me, for I am gentle and lowly in heart, and you will find rest for your souls. For My yoke *is* easy and My burden is light." (Matthew 11:28-30).

Our Lord Jesus Christ gifted us with numerous parables, principles and discourses portraying how to spiritually manage our lives. The Holy Bible is our Operations Manual.

Understanding and effectively applying the teachings of Christ will keep us on track. This will enable us to live life more fully. Without it, we frequently fall victim to a myriad of psychiatric and physical disorders. We Christians should be stress free! How many of us really experience the equanimity and quiet joy of the peace which surpasses all understanding?

In Isaiah 26:3 we read: "You will keep *him* in perfect peace, *Whose* mind is stayed *on You*, Because he trusts in You. Trust in the Lord forever." We need to totally relax under the protective power of God.

Let us also read Psalm 91: "He who dwells in the secret place of the Most High shall abide under the shadow of the Almighty. 2: I will say of the Lord, *He is* my refuge and my fortress; My God, in Him I will trust." This Psalm gives us a firm foundation for exciting, stress-free living at its very best.

It is said that about 85 percent of we Christians do not read or study our Bibles. If this is true we can be assured that this contributes to our lack of faith and empowerment. Thus the will and determination to live the teachings of Jesus is missing.

Paul, in Hebrews, comments on our lack of the most *elementary knowledge of Christianity*. Paul: "Therefore, leaving the discussion of the elementary *principles* of Christ, let us go on to perfection, not laying again the foundation of repentance from dead works and of faith toward God, of the doctrine of baptisms, of laying on of hands, of resurrection of the dead, and the eternal judgement. And this we will do if God permits." (Hebrews 6:1).

These are all matters of which we Christians should have been fully aware long ago. We need to observe those elementary elements of our Christian faith with which we are not knowledgeable. We are required to advance beyond that which Paul described as the elementary stages. The critical question is; why have we Christians not even approached the acquisition of these gifts of God, which Paul describes as elementary.

We have our seminaries, theological centres, and churches throughout the length and breadth of our land. We have trained ministers, and yet we appear only to maintain the status quo. Higher expectations than being "frozen in time" do not exist!

It is up to us as individual Christians to: "Work out your own salvation with fear and trembling; for it is God who works in you both to will and to do for His good pleasure."

"Do all things without complaining and disputing, that you may become blameless and harmless, children of God without fault in the midst of a crooked and perverse generation, among whom you shine as lights in the world, holding fast the word of life." (Philippians 2:12-15).

It is written: "And if any man thinks that he knows anything, he knows nothing yet as he ought to know." (1 Corinthians 8:2).

"For though by this time you ought to be teachers, you need *someone* to teach you again the first principles of the oracles of God; and you have come to need milk and not solid food. For everyone who partakes *only* of milk is unskilled in the word of righteousness, for he is a babe. But solid food belongs to those who are of full age, *that is*, those who by reason of use have had their senses exercised to discern both good and evil." (Hebrews 5:12-14).

We have a definite need to go right back to the elementary requisites of our belief system. "Back to basics", is the greatest tenet for golfers and sales persons, so why not for Christians and Christian leaders? We need to increase effectiveness!

However, being *natural-man* and human, we may be confronted with our egos and self-righteousness in this matter. Prayer and humility will greatly assist in an attitudinal change during our personal review.

Jesus said: "Most assuredly, I say to you, he who believes in Me, the works that I do he will do also; and greater *works* than these shall he do because I go to My Father. And whatever you ask in my name, that I will do, that the Father may be glorified in the Son. If you ask anything in My name, I will do it." (John 14:12-14).

What more do we need? That which Christ stated cannot fail! "But let him ask in faith, with no doubting, for he who doubts is like a wave of the sea driven and tossed by the wind. For let not that man suppose that he will receive anything from the Lord, he is a double-minded man, unstable in all his ways." (James 1:6-8).

Despite these two extremely powerful verses, we appear to make little or no progress in following Jesus' instructions. *What are we missing?* Do we not believe the Scriptures? Are we not committed to God?

It greatly behoves us to examine how, and if, we are applying Jesus' teachings to our everyday lives. Is this where we fail? Whatever we are doing, or not doing, is not working. It needs to be corrected.

When have we ever brought miraculous circumstances into being? We know that miracles do occur, but they are as difficult to find as rare orchids blooming in the desert.

This whole matter should have we Christians feeling quite concerned. Have we failed to obey our Lord Jesus through our disbelief in His Word? It would appear that our lack of faith and disobedience to Christ's Word calls for us to explore this sin. For sin it is. Indeed, we need to briefly explore the very nature of sin itself.

Paul's predicament in relation to sin is well known to most of us. It is our predicament too. We read in Romans: "For we know that the law is spiritual, but I am carnal, sold under sin. For what I am doing, I do not understand. For what I will to do; that I do not practice; but what I hate, that I do." (Romans 7:14-15).

Romans 7:21: "I find then a law, that evil is present with me, the one who wills to do good. 22: For I delight in the law of God according to the inward man. But I see another law in my members, warring against the law of my mind, and bringing me into captivity to the law of sin which is in my members."

We Christians shy away from the use of the word "sin". It can bring many distorted images to mind. But let us recognize that sin is a power. It primarily controls the mind of man. As Paul said, sin dwells in us, controls us and makes us do that which we should not want to do.

We are in bondage to sin. Sin creates a split in us. It is *I* who did it, but a strange *I*. It is not really our innermost self who really delights in the Word of God. Sin is in essence we self-centred entities focused on ourselves. To reiterate, sin is doing other than the will of God.

This then brings us face to face with that word *forgiveness*. To forgive is to pardon. To pardon is the excusing of an offence, [sin], without exacting a penalty.

Forgiveness or pardon is a release from the legal penalties of an offence. We are forgiven through the shed blood of our Lord Jesus Christ at the cross. He paid our penalties for us with His life.

But we need to tackle the matter of why we need forgiveness. We glibly speak of forgiveness and most us assume we know all about it!

When sin comes between God and us, it is a dark barrier. It blocks communication with our heavenly Father. Our life-lines are severed. Without spiritual input, we slowly wither away. We need to clean up our communication lines by asking God's forgiveness and guidance at least once a day! Preferably more often, as it is our nature to sin. Even a simple genuine offering of the Lord's Prayer would assist us greatly.

It is as confessed sinners that we discover that salvation is the remedy. The word *salvation* is derived from the Latin "salus", meaning to make whole and heal. Inasmuch that we are in bondage to sin, it follows that we need to be delivered from sin. We need to be liberated, to be set free!

However, there are those of us who are reticent or unaware that liberation is attainable. To awaken would require us to face up to reality and to make responsible decisions. Our life-styles may be totally changed.

"The state of being Christian requires a degree of withdrawal from the vortices of life that is lived by most of Mankind." (From the Lost Notebooks of Wiser-Mouse).

So how do we receive this salvation? The first step to becoming a Christian is to accept that Jesus died in place of us. The only way man can be saved, is through Christ choosing us. He takes our sins in substitution, so that we can be sinless in God's sight. Jesus who is the Son of God is our *bridge* to the Father.

It is written: "That if you confess with your mouth the Lord Jesus, and believe in your heart that God has raised Him from the dead, you will be saved." (Romans 10:9).

Briefly, we are saved by faith. First, we must hear the gospel, the good news of Jesus' death and resurrection.

Then we must believe, that is, fully trust our Lord Jesus. This involves repentance, a changing of mind about sin and Christ.

Christian salvation mandates acceptance of the Lord Jesus Christ. In Acts 4:12 we read: "Nor is there salvation in any other, for there is no name under heaven given among men by which we must be saved." In capsule form, we are healed and made whole. This is salvation.

However, in the light of all that our Lord Jesus Christ taught us, we and our church leaders are still stumbling in semi-darkness. Let us recall Jesus' last words on the Cross: "It is done". Yes it *IS* done. God has gifted us the plan for our salvation, and the manner in which our lives can be lived. Jesus also laid out quite explicit plans for us to enter the kingdom of heaven.

Allow us to reiterate the critical matter of wisely choosing our church and spiritual connections. We need to ensure that we are a part of the true body of Christ in an authentic Christian church. *Is our church doctrine scriptural and authentic?* Or is it a man-made religion, having a form of godliness but denying its power?

There are many churches to choose from out there. To draw an analogy, we have to recognize that "leopards", [some churches, cults and false religions], pose quite extreme danger to us. We are usually innocent and uninformed in these matters, but changes can be made!

One does not associate with leopards or condemn them because they kill. It's what leopards do! So we stay away from them. If one so chose to live or nap under a "leopard tree", that zebra or person would be accountable for his actions, in addition to suffering the deadly consequences.

We discover in Romans 6:16: "Do you not know that to whom you present yourselves slaves to obey, you are that one's slaves whom you obey, whether of sin *leading* to death, or of obedience *leading* to righteousness?" In more simple language: "To that which one yields, its servants we are." Are we yielding to Christ or to another power?

We may be cult-possessed, pseudo-Christians and not know it! This type of evil power hypnotizes untold millions of people in its black magic spell. Each of us needs to study the truths in the Holy Bible for ourselves. No one can do this for us! If we wait for the regurgitated biblical interpretations of some Christian leaders, we'll be like the little lost zebra under the leopard tree.

Again, we need to come back to survey the range of church choices with which we are confronted. Excluding the cults, some Christian churches are like black zebras with white stripes.

Whereas truly biblically-based churches are like white zebras with black stripes! The basis of differentiating between all the species is in the arrangement of the stripes, and as it is with zebras, so it is with churches.

They all seem to be so much alike! They all claim to use the same Holy Bible. Assuming that one is seeking an authentic church connection, we need to identify true Christian assemblies who emulate Christ. It is only in this way that we will we be able to learn, live, and teach what Jesus taught, with spiritual accuracy and authenticity.

We may also need to beware of those churches who hire pastors. It is the Church Board who sits in judgement on this applicant, to decide if he or she will be their shepherd. The elected church board and its rulers may be comprised mainly of "natural soul men", belonging to a pseudo-Christian church group, worshipping tradition rather than God.

Unwittingly, through general practice in the church, they may wish to mould the incoming pastor into their perpetual spiritless status quo model. An older established church at the 100 year mark, may even celebrate its anniversary as: "100 Years of Blessings!" This may be true! One wonders however, are they really only celebrating one year of pseudo-Christian experience repeated 100 times?

In all probability, the new pastor's fresh viewpoints of needed change are suppressed. His spirituality is subjected to maintaining the status quo of previous traditional, lifeless, religious practices. Of course there are many exceptions to this scenario. Much progress can be jointly effected with both parties under the guidance of the Holy Spirit.

The authentic Christian provides spiritual support in the Christian learning process. He ensures that the words of the Holy Scriptures are spiritually understood. He furthers the engrafting of the Word into the heart of the Christian. It is also critical that each of we "sheep", recognize the voice of our own shepherd.

This is much more easily said than done. We Christians of today are the end result of good, bad, indifferent or incorrect teachings by those in spiritual authority.

Thusly, we may seek to join an assembly as sincere but ignorant believers. We may be infected with incorrect spiritual baggage, in addition to corrupt Christian doctrine. *We* may well be a dangerous addition to a new church group with which we are now associating. Equally, they may be a grave danger to us.

A Christian with experience will ask a church group for its "statement of doctrine", but firstly, we need to examine exactly what we mean by Christian doctrine.

The doctrine of a Christian church refers to the body of teachings that a particular assembly believes in, and by which their lives are governed. We need to read any specific doctrinal statement carefully, for there is *sound* and *unsound* doctrine.

Ideally, we should consciously monitor how a particular church performs in actual doctrinal practise. We need to be aware of possible "sleight of hand" improprieties, or deviations from their professed doctrine.

Sound Christian doctrine refers to that body of teaching that is inspired by the Holy Spirit, and is the Holy Word of God in our Bibles. Authentic Christian doctrine must be unadulterated, that is, it must remain pure. If there is conflict in matters of doctrine, it is never a matter of *who* is right, but *what* is right, namely the Holy Scriptures.

Jesus taught the multitudes through his doctrine and his parables. He also provided the ultimate test of true doctrine. Jesus said: **"My doctrine is not Mine, but His that sent Me. If anyone wills to do His will, he shall know concerning the doctrine, whether it is from God or *whether* I speak of my own *authority*."** (John 7:16-17).

The scriptures warn us against unsound doctrine: "Now the Spirit expressly says that in latter times some will depart from the faith, giving heed to deceiving spirits and doctrines of demons, speaking lies in hypocrisy, having their own conscience seared with a hot iron, forbidding to marry, and *commanding* to abstain from foods which God created to be received with thanksgiving by those who believe the truth." (1 Timothy 4:1-3).

"For the time will come when they will not endure sound doctrine, but according to their own desires, *because* they have itching ears, they will heap up for themselves teachers; and they will turn *their* ears away from the truth, and be turned aside to fables." (2 Timothy 4:2-4).

Sound doctrine is disappearing. Most people will not tolerate it. One might ask: "What would happen if sound doctrine were being taught?" The answer is that it would be rejected! We need to recognize that it is highly possible to fall prey to alien soul predators, (pseudo-Christian type cults). This statement alone may cause us to explore the whole matter of doctrine.

Sound faith, and sound doctrine, will be the stabilizing factor in our churches. We need to associate with a church group that is scripturally correct. The great counterfeiter shall try to deceive even the very elect. If ever we are led to doubt a specific element of Christian doctrine, we need to validate the truth with the Holy Scriptures.

"Spiritual leaders with insidious doctrine closely resembling God's truth shall rise in the last days. Man's dangerous mixing of truth with error will be a primary cause of his fallen spiritual state." (From the Lost Notebooks of Wiser-Mouse).

Newcomers to Christianity of course, should not be burdened by the deep technicalities of scriptural doctrine. Nor should they be subjected to any form of commitment until they are comfortable with their scriptural beliefs. Most newcomers attend church to explore religion, interact with other families of Christians, and to make friends, and that is a good start.

Oh-Oh! Patient friend Steven wants to put a word in here!

"Like ... like ... I ain't sprouted angel wings yet ... how 'bout bringin' this Christian stuff like ... down to a level ... where a poor S.O.B. like me ... knows what you is talkin' 'bout."

"You're right Steven! O new Christian warrior! We'll just have to keep it simple!"

For starters, we need to recognize that real Christianity begins with a commitment to the teachings of Jesus. "He who has the Son has life; and he who has not the Son has not life. No man comes to the Father except through the Son." (1 John 5:12). Unless we choose to accept Jesus and to obey his commandments, there can be no impartation of eternal life, which is the subject of this whole matter.

We also have another problem that is not widely recognized! That is, we are surrounded by mass hypnosis. This is a state that resembles sleep or "living death".

The word "hypnosis" is derived from Hypnos, the Greek god of sleep. Our normal waking state of consciousness is itself a state of mental hypnosis. We are immersed in this state, just like fish in water, from birth to death.

The majority of us are totally unaware of this condition. Only rarely do we tune into the other reality fields or levels of consciousness that are available. Further, the frequency with which we tune into these other dimensions may be decades apart.

We are not all awake! Some of us may never awaken. It is certain that we will not admit to "sleeping". How could we? One has to have been asleep, and then wake up, to realize that they had been sleeping in the first place!

There are pastors also who may not be fully awake. Some are so filled with the works of religion and formalities, that they fail to go forth and live the simple teachings of Christ. God's chosen are learning too.

Those who are awake will find they are comprised of three parts. These are spirit, soul, and body. It appears that those labelled as the "living dead", believe they are of body and mind, [soul], only. So we need to explore more fully this serious business of being awake.

"Therefore He says: Awake you who sleep, Arise from the dead, And Christ will give you light." (Ephesians 5:14).

Just what did Jesus refer to when he commands us to arise from the dead? Are we not alive and talking, sipping coffee, driving, and walking around?

"Then he said to another, 'Follow Me.' But he said, 'Lord, let me go first and bury my father.' Jesus said to him, 'Let the dead bury their own dead, but you go and preach the kingdom of God'." (Luke 9:59).

There is another call to alert us to awareness: "And *do* this, knowing the time, that now *it is* high time to awake out of sleep; for now our salvation is nearer than when we *first* believed. The night is far spent, the day is at hand." (Romans 13:11-12).

Salvation is deliverance from danger, suffering and sin. It is total commitment to our Lord Jesus Christ. Note that it is, 'high time to awaken'. We'll need to examine this sleep business in some detail for it all to make sense. In a preliminary sense also, we will examine time and eternity.

Our whole concern here is with higher levels of consciousness, and what will awaken them. We possess solid bodies that exist in a world of three dimensions, and time is said to be the fourth dimension of space. We will however, not attempt an explanation of "space time"!

Suffice it to say, that "time" is one of many dimensions of space beyond that to which we are normally tuned. We humans could be compared to television or radio receiving units, with only three or four frequencies or channels in operation. The rest is static.

"Only Man's state of consciousness separates him from God. Oneness with God is the state wherein Man transcends himself. In God's presence he discovers his naked state of being. This is where Man commences his ascension." (From the Lost Notebooks of Wiser-Mouse)

It is known that an elevation in levels of consciousness will change our time sense. But for now, let us refer to the normal average human being as "time man". Maurice Nicoll in his *Living Time and the Integration of Life* gave invaluable insight on "time man" in great depth, although not within the Christian context.

"Time man" may be far along in life, well advanced in knowledge, and yet still lack understanding. Even worse, he may not have the will to live what he has comprehended. There is an incommensurable difference between what a man *knows*, and what a man *is*. A seed cannot remain a seed, and become a plant at the same time.

We Christians need to exercise boldness in our assignment as ambassadors for the kingdom. We need high self-esteem and zero self-centredness. Humility is the foundation.

We are not advocating pride, but a potent state of humility backed by quiet spiritual authority in the power of God. A man can reach a point at which he must go on and get "beyond" himself. He needs to align himself with God. No one is going to do this for him, neither church nor pastor. It is our life, and it is totally up to us! To go beyond himself, a man must *hear* and then *do* what Christ teaches. Once he is committed to authentic Christianity, he must have the will to go forward and not look back.

Our spiritual odyssey has its immutable foundation and governance in obedience. Righteousness is the offspring of obedience. Christians must never attempt to dwell in the past. To revisit sin, is sin.

"On the 'key-ring' of life, obedience to God is rooted in the engrafted Word. It is empowered by Faith, and is the only access to Salvation, the Kingdom of God, Heaven and Eternity." (From the Lost Notebooks of Wiser-Mouse).

The foundation of obedience is usually in direct conflict with man's personal sense of *"I"*. Indeed, we have found the enemy. He is *us!* Man's egocentric self, (his egoism), is normally in control of his everyday life. Self-importance is a state of immaturity. This is *natural-soul-man* supremely in control. It is the illusion of man, being a power unto himself. It is man's intent, opposing the will of God.

Man needs to attempt the process of eliminating his ego. His *"I"*, as it is diminished, is replaced with the power of the Holy Spirit. It is a slow journey for *natural-man* to become *spiritual-man*. He needs to be awake, and obedient to the promptings of the Holy Spirit. This is a Christ-like attribute of Christians growing toward maturity. It is never we as individuals who do the works of God; it is the Father within, through the Holy Spirit.

CHAPTER THREE

We need to understand this "Time-man", to whom we have alluded. He knows nothing of *"Now"*, which we are about to explore. His *"Now"*, is unwittingly a point in time on a horizontal scale. In his thinking, he is also bound primarily to *logic only*. He is always preparing for something in the future, or busy with that which occurred in his past. He may be planning additions to his world of electronic gadgetry, or perhaps an exotic trip to golden sand and turquoise water. When we do track Time-man to see if he will waken, even briefly, we find that he is in his *time-trance* state of being. He is planning for *tomorrow*, which is really an extension of *today*.

This is a time state where nothing ever "is"; something like *hope*, it is always in the future. Here is a biblical description of hope. "For we are saved in this hope, but hope that is seen is not hope; for why does one still hope for what one sees? But if we hope for what we do not see, we eagerly wait for *it* with perseverance." (Romans 8:24-25).

Firstly, however, let us explore, define, and understand our terminology. Sometime, man may, or may not, experience the dawn of "Now". [For ongoing reference "Now" will be italicized only]. We can only comprehend *Now*, by comparing that which we have seen of Time-man, who thinks only of existence in his own way. Time-man is *natural-soul-man*.

The state of *Now* is conceptually different. It is a limitless awakened state. *Now*, is a state of being; it is the experience of apprehending the space which exists above the flow of passing time. *Now* bridges worlds. It is infinitely greater than the *time* dimension.

Now contains all time, all of life, and the aeons of life. God created the aeons and the ages. It is written: "I knew you before ever the foundations of the Earth were laid."

This comprehension of *Now* is an immutable feeling of certainty that we are no longer encapsulated in "time". In *Now*, passing time halts. In this "stopping of time" one becomes a different being. One knows, sees, and feels *apart* from all other things in this approach to oneness with God. The inspired individual is elevated beyond the ego frame of mind and self. It is the spiritual state wherein the Holy Spirit can act through him.

These concepts are quite distinct from our ordinary understanding; because we basically live in the domain of Time-man and his *five senses.* This is the mental state of those who walk by "sight" only. They demand sensory proof of that which cannot be seen.

At some point, *natural-man* may perceive that everything, like truth itself, is relatively less real than that which exists immediately above it. It is only what is spiritually comprehended in *Now* that actually counts. *Now* is spiritual. Spiritual values are not associated with time. They are not in time, and their growth is not a matter of time.

Empowerment, insight, revelation, and all illumination lie in this *Now*. Higher space is timeless, and as we attempt to comprehend this *Now*, we approach the inner and holiest part of life. For in "time" all things are seeking completion, but in *Now* all things are complete. Time was made for man. Man was not made for time. Later, when we attempt to attach a linguistic description of this state, we describe it as a state of "I Am".

And God said to Moses, "I AM WHO I AM." And He said, "Thus you shall say to the children of Israel, "I AM has sent me to you." (Exodus 3:1).

"Man in absolute purity of spirit may experience oneness with God. Only rarely will his unity with God's Presence peak to the ecstatic state of 'I AM'." (From the Lost Notebooks of Wiser-Mouse).

Faith dwells in the eternal *Now*. That which Time-man understands about *faith* is something quite different. For him, every visible and earthly state and every practical approach to faith is, in the end, the negation of faith.

The word *faith* is often misunderstood to have the same meaning as *belief.* In reality, faith and belief although closely connected, are two quite different things; like two sides of a coin.

Every Christian has a measure of faith allotted to him by God. See Romans 12:3. This measure will vary from person to person, but each person's measure needs to grow. Paul, in 2 Thessalonians 1:3 told the Thessalonians that their faith had greatly grown. This increase in faith is not an intellectual or logical matter. It is spiritual. It is received from God through grace, trust, and prayer.

That which we call the present moment is not *Now*. Fleeting moments are experienced on a horizontal time-line. Frequently in our Christian world, all that is taken as *faith* belongs to the unqualified time of sleep. (By unqualified we mean unfit, not having the requisite qualifications).

Are we then really Time-man Christians only? Is this why we are so ineffective in bringing the living Word of God into reality? Is it that many Christians and even some pastors may not yet be awake? Dream states always lack the reality of commitment.

Without this *Now* state of being, all men are asleep, even the disciple, the saint or whoever. They lay like dormant pebbles in the stream of time. The future world is *not* in the future of time. It lies in another dimension.

We delay this future world by not awakening. If we could awaken, we would ascend the scale of reality concealed within us, and would understand the meaning of the future world. There is not the remotest doubt that there *is* one. Jesus spoke of: "The world to come."

It is because our future growth is in our comprehension of *Now,* and not in the tomorrow of passing-time, that something must be brought into every current moment; the cumulative effect of which is to create *Now*. While living as the *natural-man*, we must always be questing internally. Even as we go about our daily affairs, much effort has to be committed to the great quest for *Now*. It always has to be in our awareness. Time-man, despite his high intelligence does not understand this.

"Man awakened, will become acquainted with his inner-self. He will then observe the activities of his soul, and experience spiritual growth. Under the authority of Christ he becomes a 'Child of Light', impervious to powers of darkness." (From the Lost Notebooks of Wiser-Mouse).

We have a lot of work to do. The objective is to enable us to reach a new state of consciousness. This is a new state of self. It behoves us to make every effort to awaken, and depart from the world of the *living dead*.

Faith is a prime necessity to open that part of the mind *not* opened by the five senses. Spiritual knowledge cannot be communicated from one intellect to another. It must be sought for in the Spirit of God.

Let us awaken! As finite man, we may not truly understand the New Testament at all. We need to comprehend that it is constantly urging us toward these higher levels of consciousness. To live and grow toward eternity is to live and strive for unity with God. *This is our Now.*

However, let us not forget that our Lord Jesus Christ reduced his teachings to *simplicity.* Like the longest journey, it always starts with the first step. We will be drawn to examine more in-depth interpretations of the Word as we grow toward Christian maturity. Jesus commanded us to come just as we are, as innocent little children, fully trusting in Him. Later, as developing Christians, we shall learn to trust in, and rely on the Holy Spirit. We will then think as a man and not as a child.

It was A. T. Huxley who said: "Sit down before a fact like a little child, and be prepared to give up every preconceived notion, follow humbly wherever and to whatever abyss Nature leads, or you shall learn nothing." This is an excellent starting point. We will need to overcome the incorrect and distorted illusions we have of ourselves, and our world.

Above all, we need to clean house. Our heads may well be like dusty attics filled with stored grievances, spirits of darkness and death. We need to scatter the "arachnids of disbelief". They will flee in all directions under the light of God. We need to surrender to the Presence of God by *emptying* ourselves.

The Holy Scriptures are God's revelation. They let us know why men exist, and how they should live! We were not born into this world without directions. We are encouraged to grow. But note that it is up to *us.* It is not a matter of entitlement! When we have doubts, thought-action should cut in with: "We shall search the scriptures for answers."

"Man needs to recognize that he is spirit, soul, and body. The Spirit is God-given. The Soul is a living Soul. The Body is God-formed." (From the Lost Notebooks of Wiser-Mouse).

It is written: "And may your whole *spirit, soul*, and *body* be preserved blameless at the coming of our Lord Jesus Christ." (1 Thessalonians 5:23).

It really comes down to a conflict between the *forces of soul* and the *forces of the spirit*. The Children of Light can only be protected by clearly differentiating between the two. Matters pertaining to the *soul* are always directly attached to the body, which is the *natural-man*. Spiritual concerns are always related to the spirit of the man who has been *born again*. Today, more than ever before we need to: "Test all things; hold fast what is good. Abstain from every form of evil." (1 Thessalonians 5:21).

We have further cause for concern, when we read in Revelation, that there is a trading of human bodies, [slaves]. There is also a *merchandising of the souls of men.* Those who are not in Christ are merely a commodity which is traded. As yet, most Christians do not recognize this fact! How did this come about? Are we operating as a commodity under Satan, or are we operating as sons of God under the guidance of the Holy Spirit?

The highest attainment in Christianity is that of complete spiritual union between God and man. Christian miracles are performed by God through the Holy Spirit. God does not work through man's soul-power. He works through man's spirit-power. When we are *born-again*, we are born of the Holy Spirit. This means we have awakened and are in the spirit.

However, we need to be aware that astounding miracles will be performed by Man through his *soul-self*. Positive thinking groups teach that: "Whatever the mind of man can conceive, he can achieve." This is true, even to the point of deceiving the very elect. In actuality, they are proclaiming: "Everything comes from *us,* not from *God.*" Indeed, serpents are wise and Christians are naïve.

We now need to establish a foundation for authentic Christians, in the matter of judging Christian leadership. We normally accept the doctrines and teaching of our leaders and pastors without question. The fact that we may act in a judgemental capacity in the church, is an alien concept to most of us. It is almost unthinkable! We may even be seen as rebellious, and in defiance of God's appointed authority.

Guy Duininck in his *True or False—Judging Doctrine and Leadership* states: "Learning how to judge doctrine and spiritual leadership will save believers and local churches from spiritual disaster."

Further, he states: "Unlearned, unstable and wrongly-motivated individuals will continue to secure positions of spiritual leadership." He comes up with words of encouragement too: "You are not only permitted to judge, but you are also responsible and capable of judging in these areas."

We need to understand this whole matter of judgement. We Christians are usually stricken speechless when confronted with that which should be challenged, be it of doctrine or otherwise.

We may not be equipped to handle deviant doctrine. We may unwittingly allow departures from that which is Scriptural. We must not condone doctrinal differences with silence and acquiescence. This is a recurring problem.

A well-known biblical quote is: "Judge not, that you be not judged. For with what judgement you judge, you will be judged; and with the measure you use, it will be measured back to you." (Matthew 7:1-2).

We understand that we should not judge, criticize or condemn. In these three words we find the kind of judging that believers must *not* do. However, it *is* scriptural for Christians to judge. This is an element of Christian organizational structure that is not widely recognized. It is known as "objective judging". It is an allowable and expected spiritual activity. It originates with the Holy Spirit. He who is *"natural-soul-man"* only, does not possess the spiritual power or comprehension to intrude in this area.

We discover in 1 Corinthians 2:15: "But he who is spiritual judges all things, yet he himself is *rightly* judged by no one. *For who has known the mind of the Lord that he may instruct Him?* But that we have the mind of Christ."

There is a significant difference between judging with a self-righteous and critical attitude, and judging based on a sincere desire to maintain spiritual integrity. This latter type of judging, is what the Word of God encourages us to *do.* It is that judging which means to weigh, to discern, search out, access and evaluate teachers and teaching to determine their true spiritual value.

We will need to monitor reasons for exercising objective judgement. Something may have caught our attention and triggered us to examine a particular issue. We may have identified erroneous doctrine, or some other off-track Christian matter. Firstly, we submit our concern in prayer to our heavenly Father. We then await that which the Holy Spirit imparts us, from the Father. Our self and our egoism are in no way involved.

We may have encountered a well-meaning, dedicated, but not God-connected pastor, who prays in an off-hand, casual manner. This is where the pastor's message, tone and prayers, are the same as if he had quickly said to one of his children: "After that, go and clean up your room. We ask this in the name of your Son. Amen."

We may have been struck with the lack of awe and reverence. Where is the *fear* of the Lord, the ultimate respect? Do they not realize that in true prayer they are in the very Presence of God? Through Christ, do they not have a direct spiritual relationship with our heavenly Father? One senses the indwelling of the Holy Spirit is missing. Much of that which is presented may be *soul-logic*. Christians who are indwelt of the Holy Spirit are keenly aware of this.

A minister of God may possess a document that certifies him to be a pastor; however this does not mean that he is ordained of God. We need to pray for our pastors. Theirs is not an easy life. They too, are still growing in spiritual comprehension.

True ministry is God-touched, God-enabled, and God-made. The preaching man has to be ordained of God to be effective. This anointing makes God's truth powerful and interesting. It draws, attracts and edifies. It convicts and saves. It is an anointing. *It is not soul-based intellectualism.*

"For the word of God *is* living and powerful, and sharper than any two-edged sword, piercing even to the division of soul and spirit, and joints and marrow, and is a discerner of the thoughts and intents of the heart. And there is no creature hidden from His sight, but all things *are* naked and open to the eyes of Him to whom we *must give account.*" (Hebrews 4:12-13).

We need to ask ourselves why people come to our church, or to any other church for that matter. Is it possible for us to think that we draw them to us, like being drawn by the wafts of hot fresh smells from the bakery up the road? The attraction of the all-pervading delicious aroma of coffee being ground at a nearby plant, is equally irresistible. These draw us.

Are we enabling the healing of the sick through Christ physically and psychologically? Has the Word gone out into the community of the power residing in our particular assembly? Let us be assured that if it had, there would be traffic control problems throughout the entire area. Do we recognize our accountability in providing insight on the day to day problems of our congregations?

"Steven! You're getting real "antsy". What are you looking it? Remember that your binoculars bring things fifteen times closer than they really are!"

"I like what you was sayin' like … but you better … check out your rifle … I'm seein' a problem we may have to solve like …"

Steve had spotted a female grizzly with two cubs, a scant quarter kilometre away. With the wind facing us, there was no immediate cause for concern. But I quit writing and joined Steve. For the next forty minutes, it was with delight that we watched the little grizzlies chasing around and tussling with each other.

As the scene unfolded, the bears appeared to be scarily close, and due to the grizzlies' proximity we decided to relocate. As yet, we had never found ourselves in a position where we had to use a rifle in self-defence with any of God's creations.

When we returned to the *Wiser-Mouse Legacy* the following day, our minds were still filled with grizzly bear images. Moments with wild creatures in the wilderness stay with one forever.

To return to "why people come to our church", our business is the equipping of *future saints* to manage life effectively. This is a daunting process. The Holy Spirit will guide us in all truth to achieve that for which we pray in faith.

In many Protestant churches, the word "saint" is used to refer to anyone who is a Christian. This is similar to Paul's numerous references in the New Testament; in the sense that anyone who is truly in the Body of Christ and a professing Christian is a saint. We concur with Paul's statements, in the light of referring to authentic Christians in particular. But note how indistinct the varied meanings of *saint* can be. A scale of two is vastly different from a scale of say, nine, in recognizing a spirit-filled saint being effective in his mission.

Are we providing our congregations with Christian know-how; in facing such challenges as lost employment, financial woes, illness, depression and relationship breakdowns? These generally have severe psychological repercussions.

Just who are these people who show up at our church? What are they seeking? For what are they hungering? Will they find it in our assembly? Did we physically or spiritually feed them? [Feed my lambs]. Did we give them hope? Or did they leave confused and hungry for solutions to what may appear to them to be overwhelming problems.

At times, we tend to appear to be offended by the type of persons who enter our assemblies. Maybe it is their appearance, or what we see in their eyes.

Let us take a look at our church through the eyes of a newcomer. A lone guy walks in, sits down and watches. He goes through the service in a tolerant and restrained manner, but he is a little uncomfortable at times.

He may have the courage to stay for fellowship and coffee after the service. Will he find other church-goers so wrapped up in their own animated chatter and laughter, that they pay him only an occasional furtive glance? He may feel that nobody really cares. (Despite denial, this is reality).

Did we somewhat *offended Christians* not read in the scriptures, that Jesus was soundly criticized when he sat and dined with thieves, sexual deviants, murderers and other undesirable types? Did He retreat from people with evil life-styles with an offended "holier than thou" attitude? How did He handle it? Why can we not do likewise?

"When Jesus heard *it*, He said to them, 'Those who are well have no need of a physician, but those who are sick. I did not come to call the righteous, but sinners, to repentance'" (Mark 2:17).

The fact remains, that we are all the sum total of our experiences, and the power we now possess lies in how we have dealt with life's situations. Some of us may have developed into entities of extraordinary resilience and power, even more so, with Jesus as our established foundation. [Paul] "I can do all things through Christ who strengthens me." (Philippians 4:13).

Maybe that lone guy who came to our church, needed to explore answers to his problems. Perhaps he is now one of thousands who will not return. Church portrayed for him a future dream world of crowns and songs about victory. After he is dead, nice things will happen. How disillusioned and off-track he must feel!

What about now? "This is *me*. I'm alive *now*. I'm hurting. I need help and don't know how to ask for it. I'm desperate. Can you not hear my silent screams? Why are you so detached and unfeeling? Hello there! Are *you* the dream or am I?"

Was he welcomed by one of the elders upon arrival, and in private, was he counselled by that elder in relation to his spiritual and physical needs? Or, was he more or less ignored when the assembly broke up for fellowship and refreshments?

"In fear, Man draws a circle of protection around himself to keep love out. In love, God draws a circle around Man, and brings him in!" (From the Lost Notebooks of Wiser-Mouse).

"What's that Steve?"

"Like ... man ... that poor s.o.b ... lookin' for help ... sounds a lot like you when you was down and out!"

"Yes Steven, that is true."

Maybe we failed to help him. How many others lower down on the scale of need did we also unwittingly reject? Are we mesmerized by our church activities and schedules? Do we not have the time? Or do we feel threatened by our *own* inadequacies? Are we equipped to face and manage the "realities" that may walk in?

What may they find? Most newcomers need understanding, wisdom and inspiration. Others merely need a meal, and this will be handled in line with the church's established policy.

(A policy is *not* a rule or regulation, although it is often thrust into that context. It is a guideline to manage situations that repetitively occur. It possesses discretional flexibility).

Everything depends on the spiritual character of the Christian leader. The preaching that kills is unspiritual preaching. The power of the message may not be God-inspired.

Some sermons are dry and discursive, and tragically, they contain not one iota of peripheral "waking-power". The people remain physically or spiritually asleep, fulfilling their misguided duty of being in church.

We *are* suggesting that we need to return to the basics of providing Christian methods, know-how, and power, to solve the difficulties of life. This is not only our duty, but our accountability and joy in Christ. *This is authentic Christianity in action!*

Now, let us take a look around us. Traffic is rushing to and fro as we rise in the morning. We are gripped with the obsession of converting time into money to pay for endless wants. Maybe it's true that a person whose wants and needs are few, is rich indeed! Homes are acquired, along with cars, trucks, and trailers.

We pay mortgages, go on exotic vacations, play golf, attend concerts, and generally involve ourselves in relationships. We even try to keep our credit cards under control! We raise kids, and all the while we plan for a future which never comes, because it is always our *present*. This is the life of Time-man.

We read in Ecclesiastes 1:2: "Vanity of vanities, said the Preacher; vanity of vanities, all is vanity." Solomon is also suggesting that we *awaken.* King Solomon, the writer of Ecclesiastes who had wealth beyond imagination, said that:

"Life under the sun, lived as though all there is to life is what we can experience through sight, taste, touch, smell and hearing, is *meaningless.*"

"Man dies internally if he lacks recognition of spiritual values, purpose and direction." (From the Lost Notebooks of Wiser-Mouse).

Many lives tend to be generally devoid of purpose. We do not ask such primary questions as: "Why are we here?" or "What is life all about?" We endure, or try to escape from the experiences of our everyday lives. We are unaware that we are immersed in a living dream-state of illusion.

Meaning and purpose in life should originate in childhood as part of parenting. But as individuals, we all have to learn life's lessons from square one, as did our parents. On this foundation of assumed equivalency, we grow, or never awaken. Were our parents *awake*, maybe we would have been correctly blueprinted too.

Why is there such a void in our comprehension? God created us for something beyond what we can experience in the here-and-now. Solomon said of God: *"He has set Eternity in the hearts of men."* In our hypnotic state, we see nothing wrong with living in our current void. But our recurring question needs to be, why do we struggle with this reality of existing among the living dead? Yes! Again we refer to the *living dead!*

Of course, the answer is that we may not have as yet been *born of the spirit*. We have all heard ad nauseam about being "born again". Those of us who have attained this state are frequently referred to in disgust as: "He's one of those 'born again' Christians. God help us!"

There are two biblical verses that may give us a more in-depth, wide-angle view of God and spiritual concerns. "For My thoughts *are* not your thoughts, nor *are* your ways My ways," says the Lord. "For as the heavens are higher than the earth, So are My ways higher than your ways, and My thoughts than your thoughts." (Isaiah 55:8-9).

Also in John 8:23: "And He said unto them, 'You are from beneath; I am from above. You are of this world; I am not of this world."

This should give us needed self-perspective. Indeed, only a few of us have gazed far into the cosmos at night, and been overwhelmed with the vastness of our universe. In the cities, man-made lights obscure the stars and planets. But on a clear night in the hills, one can see *forever.* One cannot look into the night sky, and not be entranced with wonderment and deep feelings of humility.

Our blue planet Earth orbits within one of the smaller galaxies. Are we the only life form even in our small galaxy? Let us remove our blinders and awaken to reality. God's thoughts are light years above our pathetic, self-centred level of thinking. Our God is devoid of our self-imposed limitations. All things are possible with God. The entire Universe is within our one, living God. He is "I AM".

"In this life, Man can only reach God through love, never by thought or knowledge." (From the Lost Notebooks of Wiser-Mouse).

"Steven! You look concerned about something, I can tell. What's up?"

"Like ... them grizzlies wc just seen ... they is ... again headed our way like ... for a short while ... we could say we is the livin' dead like ... unless we get out this area right now!"

So once again we relocated, and never saw those particular grizzlies again. True to the laws of wilderness survival, we set up camp for the night and made a big fire. In fact, for two whole days, we did not continue with the *Wiser-Mouse Legacy.* We just lazed around, fished, and stuffed ourselves with rainbow trout. We quenched our thirst with creek water and Heinekens.

On the matter of humans and why we are here, there is no better work on "purpose in life", than Rick Warn's; *The Purpose Driven Life* and its twin volume, *The Purpose Driven Church.* To gain true perspective on life, these two books are right at the top in their influence on practical, attainable Christianity. We need to read them again and again, and then start *living* them!

We have to start somewhere in our search for true meaning and purpose in life. I can think of no better way than to bring to mind a question from my seven year old grandson. "Granpa! How do I talk to God?" A child can ask questions that a wise man may not be able to answer. Out of the mouths of babes! Oh boy! How do we handle this one? How do we teach kids about real life with belief and faith in action?

What came to mind as a method of explanation, were the myriad of Bible story books with pretty pictures of Jesus in the manger, surrounded by the animals and the three wise men. Then, there are the stories about David and Goliath, Daniel in the lion's den, and numerous others. But these books seemed to be devoid of any spiritual explanation.

God's spiritual power in the Bible stories is available to our kids now, as they grow in the spirit. But the linkage to spiritual power in these books is often reduced to myth and fable. It is wrong to assume that kids are too young to understand matters of the spirit. It is not the case.

Truly, these kids are the little children spoken of by Christ physically, mentally and spiritually.

Children are small in comprehension. They have innocent minds, open and clear for receptivity. Their minds are like old-fashioned photographic plates awaiting images. They are filled with belief and trust. This is a sacred dimension of purity that is not to be violated. This is where we start building our Godly relationships. Is this where we also start talking *with* God? Yes!

It is no wonder that Jesus came down so strongly on those who corrupted, or defiled, the minds of the little children. Jesus says: "Whosoever causes one of these little ones who believe in Me to sin, it would be better for him if a millstone were hung around his neck, and he were drowned in the depth of the sea." (Matthew 18:6).

Jesus knew that children are more open to the divine Presence than we adults.

In Matthew 18:3 He said: "Assuredly, I say to you, unless you are converted and become as little children, you will by no means enter the kingdom of heaven."

The term "little children", is often misrepresented as applying to kids only. In reality, it also refers to those adults who are "small in understanding". Adults must come with conscious innocence, and an open mind, in order to accept the scriptures without a lot of logic and reasoning.

That's a lot to ask! The difference being; that the "adult little children", will have a great deal of ego-garbage, bias, and incorrect teaching with which to contend. Much of this conditioning will need to be erased and overcome. This will make their journey more challenging. Immature child-adults must avoid inflicting unwitting damage to the spiritual comprehension of others.

Once I have my innocent grandchildren launched into spirituality, there is the need to warn them about the *false forms of Christianity*. They should be alerted to identify those assemblies who are deeply involved with traditions, even though they use our regular Bibles.

World-wide media coverage has reinforced many distorted scriptural falsehoods in the minds of the populace. Indeed, media power frequently portrays Christianity as quite the opposite of what our Lord Jesus Christ taught.

Our sufficiency is from God, nothing comes from us. The words of Jesus to His disciples were: "For without Me, you can do nothing." (John 15:5).

We must also be aware of the Bible critics, who devote volumes of printed material in attempts to refute its teachings. The Scriptures will never yield their spiritual insight, beauty and elegance to those who are imprinted with the need for step-by-step logical scientific proof. "God *is* Spirit, and those who worship Him must worship in spirit and truth." (John 4:24).

That which is below, must obey that which is above. We live in a spiritual unseen dimension. Our level of logic can never penetrate that level which is spiritual. The scriptures do not change. "Heaven and earth shall pass away, but My word shall not."

Saint Augustine said: "If you believe what you like in the gospels, and reject what you don't like, it is not the gospel you believe, but yourself."

Relevant scriptures are like gold nuggets. All the hard panning for gold has been done. These nugget-references are essential to our biblical understanding. We often need to call upon them. In 2 Timothy 3:16 we are instructed that: "All Scripture *is* given by inspiration of God, and *is* profitable for doctrine, for reproof, for correction, for instruction in righteousness, that the man of God may be complete, thoroughly equipped for every good work."

There is another wonderful promise that we receive when we accept our Lord Jesus Christ. He has declared that: "For assuredly, I say to you, till heaven and earth pass away, one jot or one tittle will by no means pass from the law till all is fulfilled." (Matthew 5:18). These are Jesus' guarantees. The Scriptures cannot be broken!

Another equally beautiful promise is found in John 14:13: "And whatever you ask in My name, that I will do, that the Father may be glorified in the Son. 14: If you ask anything in My name, I will do it."

How about that for sheer spiritual elegance! We can feel the immutable power of God in motion. We are assured that every prophecy will be fulfilled, and that He is in charge of eternity. We use the term *elegance* here, in the same way that cosmic physicists describe their equations in explaining the universe. They find them to be of such elegance in design and perfection that even *they* stand in awe before God's creation!

When the authentic Christian seriously studies his Bible and attempts to discuss it with his friends, he may be met with a high degree of scoffing and ridicule. The Bible is well ahead of these commentators, as well as those who misguidedly or deliberately mislead others in spiritual matters. We are warned against false prophets, seducing spirits and strange doctrines. Further we are instructed not to be tossed to and fro by every wind of new doctrine.

The authentic Christian is an ambassador for Christ. "The Spirit Himself bears witness with our spirit that we are children of God, and if children, then heirs, heirs of God and joint heirs with Christ, if indeed we suffer with Him, that we may also be glorified together." (Romans 8:16-17).

A son of God has responsibilities of an awesome nature. He is accountable to God and man for his thoughts, words and actions. *He has received powers of a type that are unprecedented on earth.* His powers include the raising of the dead, to heal all manner of disease including his own, and to gift the blind with sight.

More astoundingly, he has the power and ability to *bind or loose* circumstances on earth and in heaven. Elijah's binding and loosing of rain in 2 Kings 17:1, is but one example among many of those working in liaison with God.

Let us take to heart in Matthew 16:19: "And I will give to you the keys of the kingdom of heaven, and whatever you bind on earth will be bound in heaven, and whatever you loose on earth will be loosed in heaven."

"Man's failure to abdicate his 'throne-of-self', negates his spiritual power to 'bring things into being that were not'." (From the Lost Notebooks of Wiser-Mouse).

In following the commands of Christ, we are also empowered to cast out devils or unclean spirits. They are still with us today. This is not a matter of "that was then and this is now". Many persons are indwelt by evil spirits as much today, as they were two thousand years ago. In dealing with evil spirits we need to be indwelt by the Holy Spirit and follow His promptings.

We now need to briefly touch on initial approaches to prayer, wherein our greatest need is to petition our heavenly Father in regard to our being cleansed of sin. A red flag should be waved here! Our communication lines with God are frequently as, "free-flowing as a blocked drain".

In John 6:44 Jesus says: "No one can come to Me unless the Father who sent Me draws him; and I will raise him up at the last day."

In Matthew 23:9 we are instructed: "Do not call anyone on earth your Father; for One is your Father, He who is in heaven."

It is written, that when we pray, we pray to the Father in the name of Jesus. The Bible does *not* tell us to pray to Jesus *directly* as some Christians do. Many Christians say this does not matter because they are all a part of the Tri-Unity. However this negates the specific *roles* of each member of the Godhead, even though they are *one.* The Godhead will always recognize the *intent* of heart, versus misinformation, but error is not a licence to sin under grace.

Petitioning, and making specific requests to Jesus directly is *not* scriptural. If we *bend* the Scriptures here, we are already in quick-sand. It is not a matter of semantics or splitting-hairs as is so often stated. We are commanded to ask of the Father in Jesus' name. (Our text will enlarge on this a little later).

Christ did not teach confusion, but misinterpretation appears to reign in that which man has made of Jesus' sovereignty and His teachings. Are we missing some of the basics? For example, throughout Christianity there is a great unrecognized need for clarification of what individual spiritual progress is all about.

Man, spiritually imbalanced, falls prey to the status quo of slow Christian growth. There may be too heavy an emphasis on "making a joyful noise unto the Lord". The singing of hymns is primarily recognized as worship. It is referred to as the worship-portion of the service. However, worship takes many other forms including Bible study.

Individual spiritual growth needs to come under scrutiny. We reiterate; we need to study Paul's statements on that which he describes as *elementary!* (Hebrews 6:1-3). We Christians need to discover, perhaps for the first time, the *elementary teachings of Christianity.*

We also have to learn the effective application of the life principles that Christ taught. The power of the tongue needs to be fully understood. We need to become word-conscious, before we speak!

Mature Christians automatically screen observations of that which is being heard or spoken. A quite elementary example, is hearing a phrase that is commonly used within the Christian community. It is said in regard to many of the activities within the church that we: "Do things for God". Most would never give this a second thought. However, this whole idea of "Doing things for God", is an alien concept to authentic Christianity. It is unwittingly, a simple, self-oriented, egotistical statement.

Acting in obedience to the Holy Spirit, yes, but it is not within the causal-cognition of spiritual-man to envision himself at any time as "doing things for God". It is God through grace who "does things for men".

This word-awareness is a central-focus that slowly develops, as one experiences progress toward Christian maturity. It is part of the monitoring process initiated by our Gatekeeper, about whom we will learn more about shortly. In the final analysis, it is up to the individual Christian to obey that which the Holy Spirit reveals to him.

Authentic Christians are Children of Light. "Every good gift and every perfect gift is from above, and comes down from the Father of lights, with whom there is no variation or shadow of turning." (James 1:17).

We need to recognize and acknowledge the simplicity in authentic Christianity: "*There is* one body, and one Spirit, just as you were called in one hope of your calling; one Lord, one faith, one baptism, one God and Father of all, who is above all, and through all, and in you all." (Ephesians 4:4-6).

We must not lose sight of that which we seek in all matters pertaining to Scriptural truth. We are still in quest of an answer to our most basic of Christian challenges:

"If the Christian teaching and practise in our churches is so right, what makes Christians of today so ineffective, so impotent, and so utterly powerless in the face of all the spiritual principles that Jesus taught?"

We have already seen that Christianity as currently practiced, is a confusion of denominations and man-made demonic heresies. Still others are *natural-man's* corrupt attempt to translate that which is spiritual, into human *logic*. They are portrayals of man's ego, empowered by Satan, the prince of this world, attempting to override the Word of God.

Of all that has been sown or planted either by religious coercion, or free-will, what do we plainly see, and experience? What are the end-results, [fruit], of all the pomp and ceremony of the religions that we habitually condone and accept? *What is this religious surreal evidence that so blatantly faces us?*

It is Christianity as generally practised, spurious, powerless, and void of progress! It is this abysmal failure that few

Christians or their leaders care to acknowledge. The formula seems to be: "Maintain the status quo through repetition of habit and tradition". Or, "Play it safe for financial reasons." These formulae are the route to eternal death. Why do we Christians not question this doctrine? This treatise simply submits evidence of that which is open for all to see, but it is of special significance to those Christians with with "opened eyes", indwelt by the Holy Spirit. In growing toward spiritual maturity, we all are accountable to God. Our fruits are seen through the eyes of God. It is written that by our fruits are we known. This applies to churches and to pastors.

It has long been proven that darkness flees before light. We only have to take a multi-million candle power lamp out in the dark of night, to see this occur. Switch on the lamp, and the darkness we may have feared recedes before us as we walk. "Let your light so shine before men, that they may see your good works, and glorify your Father in heaven." (Matthew 5:16).

In the same manner, as Children of Light, as we walk in the Spirit, darkness must recede. It is a law of God. It is upheld and maintained by God. It cannot be otherwise. The pivotal question is; what is powering our lamps? Are they bright enough to cause darkness to flee before us? Are we ensuring that our lamps are fully charged at all times? Our lamps are powered by the Word of God. Let us remember that: *Fear brings Satan on the scene. Faith brings God on the scene.*

We need to strengthen our faith, and we can, almost to the point of walking on air! We can feel encouraged, secure and protected when we read any part of Psalm 91.

"He who dwells in the secret place of the Most High shall abide under the shadow of the Almighty. 2: I will say of the Lord, *He is* my refuge and my fortress: My God, in Him will

I trust. 3: Surely he shall deliver you from the snare of the fowler, *and* from the noisy pestilence.

4: He shall cover you with His feathers, and under His wings you shall take refuge; His truth *shall be your* shield and buckler. 5: You shall not be afraid of the terror by night, Nor of the arrow *that* flies by day; 6: Nor for the pestilence *that* walks in darkness; nor for the destruction *that* lays waste at noonday.

7: A thousand may fall at your side, and ten thousand *at* your right hand; *But* it shall not come near you. 8: Only with your eyes shall you look, and see the reward of the wicked.

9: Because you have made the Lord, who is my refuge, *Even* the Most High, your dwelling place, 10: No evil shall befall you, Nor shall any plague come to your dwelling. 11: For he shall give his angels charge over you, to keep you in all your ways.

15: He shall call upon Me, and I will answer him; *I will be* with him in trouble; I will deliver him, and honour him. 16: With long life will I satisfy him, and show him My salvation.

Our heavenly Father will never leave us or forsake us. He is with us to end of the World.

"The Word of God engrafted in the heart of Man is a fountain of love, trust and peace. Devoid of fear, Man is a beacon of light. He dwells in the parallel worlds of soul and spirit in harmony with God." (From the Lost Notebooks of Wiser-Mouse).

CHAPTER FOUR

"For God has not given us a spirit of fear, but of power and of love and of a sound mind." (2 Timothy 1:7).

This now brings us to the critical matter of the thoughts that invade our minds, and from where they originate. Thoughts and attitudes are the authors of fear, depression, illness and poverty, among a myriad of other negative physical and mental factors. Conversely, we know that the offspring of positive thoughts can yield good health, financial well-being, and living life abundantly as Christ taught.

Did we fail to get a good night's rest? The troubles of the day need no rest, and we brought them to bed with us. Dwelling on negative thoughts is generally known as worrying. But, is this mode of thinking produced by a sound mind? Further, what is a sound mind? It is a mind not governed by fear! It is a fear-free mind under the direction of the Holy Spirit.

We have as yet to learn how to control the demand our unsolved problems place upon us. We allow them to rule us. For a start, it would help if we consciously formulated "phrases of responsibility". For example: "I allowed myself to get quite upset." Or: "I permitted myself to become very hurt." These are statements of transparency, and would indicate that one had some form of conscious control of one's self.

Regardless of the problems with which we are confronted, note that we need to place the responsibility for our reactions to those problems on *us.* It is a matter of self-control.

We need to bear in mind, that both negative and positive thinking, originate with the earthly *natural-man*. They are born out of walking by *sight* only. Both *natural-man* and Time-man being the the same, operate primarily from their souls, and logic. The thinking mode of authentic Christians is a spiritually-based higher level of consciousness.

Faith is the substance of things hoped for, and reaches into the realm of the spirit and manifests the promises of God. Fear is the substance of things not desired, and reaches into the unseen realm to manifest the threats of the devil. We reiterate that the shield of the engrafted Word is: "F*ear brings Satan on the scene. Faith brings God on the scene.*"

It has to be our conscious choice. Christians are empowered to be in control. We were not thrown into the vortices of life to sink or swim in a violent maelstrom of uncontrollable circumstances. Nor were we committed to depression and its orchestration of disease symptoms. "Many *are* the afflictions of the righteous, But the Lord delivers him out of them all." (Psalm 34:19).

"Be anxious for nothing, but in everything by prayer and supplication, with thanksgiving, let your requests be made known to God; and the peace of God, which surpasses all understanding, will guard your hearts and minds through Christ Jesus." (Philippians 4:6-7).

This peace brings with it an era of stress-free living. It will largely negate the deadly effects of the unrelenting tension on our physical bodies. We may not as yet have formulated thought as to how, or when, we are going to manage our recurring problems. The truth is that few of us have ever been free of them. Even under crushing conditions, soul-searching questions have to be asked. It is a necessary part of our personal assessment.

It is said that one in ten North Americans live in psychological depression. We live in a desert of spiritual ignorance and darkness. It inundates most of us, whether we call ourselves Christians or not. Masses of soul-based psychologists, psychiatrists, counsellors, and psycho-pharmacologists, struggle to relieve our psychic torture with its debilitating pain. Their efforts are genuine, and their intent to heal is undeniable.

We may well ask; where is the all-encompassing *spiritual element?* The field of psychology is basically soul-based. These professionals rarely enter the spiritual-realm; and have been primarily educated by the institutions of higher learning, not to think "outside of the box". Their programming is the unchallenged intellectualism of man, a lot of which is over one hundred years old. It is time-based, whereas, that which is spiritual, is outside of time, and lies within eternity. Neither God, nor Christian spiritual knowledge can ever become outdated.

If we practice only a *soul-based* form of Christianity, our claims to empower healing of the whole man through our heavenly Father, is no further ahead than is psychology. Whatever it is that we sow; it is that which we reap.

We need to give serious thought to the matter of where depressing and damaging thoughts originate. How do they gain entry to seize the power by which they sabotage our minds and our lives?

Authentic Christians are usually consciously aware of when alien forces have accessed their thought-processes. They have the ability to take appropriate action and eliminate them. These invasions and infiltrations are similar to our computer viruses. The familiar "Trojan horse" virus lies dormant after gaining entry.

Only later, does it release the destructive elements from its belly cavity, with devastating results. The computer may *crash*. But in our human psyche-systems, we well may die both physically, and spiritually. So how do these deadly elements gain entry?

It is *we* who answer the knock on the door to our minds, and whom do we find standing there? An invisible messenger in raiment of light! We have already acquiesced through lack of knowledge to accept the offerings of this alien. Our minds are operating on auto-pilot. Therefore, unwittingly, it is *we* who allow entry of these deadly intruders. No *aliens* were ever required to identify their mission. This uncharted no-man's-land is accessible to all. Are there no established boundaries?

It's a little like opening up a box we have just received from some courier. The door is always open, so couriers have free delivery access. Here's another package, let's accept it and open it. It could contain killer bees! But no, it is far worse! These insidious marauders escaping from the box are like viruses. They are unseen elemental thought-forms, operating on different wavelengths. They cannot be seen, heard, smelled, tasted, or touched, and are not felt. *Not as yet.*

We will discover eventually, that these thought-forms are mainly words that originated from our own tongues. These are a myriad of unchecked evil thoughts that have come back to haunt us in Satanic forms. They will dominate our life attitude, our health, and immunity to disease. In addition, they negate our ability to prosper in relationships, and finances.

They have been authorized and empowered to work against us. They suck the life out of us and continue to do so!

Worse still, can we believe it? It is *we* who authorized and empowered them! How can this be?

We have yet to appoint a specific "gatekeeper", whose duty it would be to check passports, before allowing or denying any alien spirit force from attempting to invade our soul's inner sanctum. When this breach in security occurs, it inevitably leads to total contamination. Our soul or *natural-man,* in addition to our spiritual selves, has become adulterated. (Truth mixed with error).

Note the word "appoint". It is connected to *us* and to *our will.* It is we who through salvation consciously appoint this "Gatekeeper". He is known to us. We are part of Him. He is our Lord Jesus Christ. "Casting down arguments and every high thing that exalts itself against the knowledge of God, bringing every thought into captivity to the obedience of Christ." (2 Corinthians 10:5).

Will we deny ourselves access to God's kingdom? No way! Do we change now or later?

"The greatest demand that God's Word places on Man is for him to obey. Obedience is absolutely honouring God, for it alone acknowledges God's Will as its centre." (From the Lost Notebooks of Wiser-Mouse).

Most Christians have never considered a thought-screening process, or any other method of mental discipline. We have identified the Gatekeeper as the Word of God, and that the Word is the screen, or filter, through which our lives are to be directed.

We shudder at the word "discipline". It means effort on our part. However, it appears that we have hit the jackpot! We need self-discipline! Oh no! Oh! Yes!

"Steven, why the frowns? What's happening to you?"

"Like ... easy there like! We're not Bible heroes ... give us some breathin' space like! You got the reigns so tight like ... my jaws is bleedin' ..."

"Okay Steve, we'll ease-up, but nothing changes! We still need to develop ourselves. This is a life and death matter. It's like you, warning me that the wind has changed direction, and those grizzlies up front are now getting our full scent. In which case, maybe we'll be in deep trouble. Sure, I can ignore the warning, but later I may also have to pay the price."

"Like ... okay ... maybe I'll have to ... like ... take the *Wiser-Mouse Legacy* in smaller chewable chunks like ..."

"Steve, I believe you're right! We're back at the starting gate! This is one tall order, even for authentic Christians!"

We will need patience. By degrees, the Gatekeeper will automatically screen all incoming images, data and messages. It's like passport inspection! The inspector is the superimposed Word of God.

Self-discipline will be a part of what really is our operating-system. This is the software system of the engrafted Word. The manual for that system is our Holy Bible.

Authentic Christians have an invisible force-field surrounding them. They have light, peace, grace, and power emanating from within. People can feel the peace and love that Christians project. They want that frame of mind.

The Scriptures tell us that: "Death and life are in the power of the tongue, And those who love it will eat its fruit." (Proverbs 18:21). Note that it does not say *life and death,* but the other way round.

"Even so the tongue is a little member, and it can boast of great things. See how much wood or how great a forest a tiny spark can set ablaze! And the tongue *is* a fire." (Amplified Bible. James 3:5-6). "But the human tongue can be tamed by no man. It is restless [undisciplined, irreconcilable] evil, full of deadly poison." (Amp. James 3:8).

This is reality hitting us amidships! We are to attempt to control our tongues! The words we speak are alive with the potent power of death and life. Our tongues prophesy poverty, or wealth, health, or sickness, effective living, or the evil weight of depression. When we speak, we have choices. We can launch fiery flaming darts of destruction, or, as true ambassadors for Christ, we can launch words of love, acceptance, grace, hope, and healing. We always have a choice.

"Throughout life, every word and prayer that Man utters will shape his destiny." (From the Lost Notebooks of Wiser-Mouse).

We are further admonished: "But I say to you that every idle word that men may speak, they will give account of it in the day of judgement." (Matthew 12:36).

Here are three more gold nuggets!

"For by your words you will be justified, and by your words you will be condemned." (Matthew 12:37).

"Not that which goes into the mouth defiles a man; but what comes out of the mouth, this defiles a man." (Matthew 15:11).

"It is written: "Man shall not live by bread alone, but by every word that proceeds from the mouth of God." (Matthew 4:4).

When we speak to our heavenly Father in Faith through Jesus, the words formed by our tongues, and spoken by us, will act in obedience to God's spiritual laws.

The sad truth is that we are victims of our own negative self-fulfilling prophesies. Our words are frequently spoken negatively from *soul-force.* A typical example may be: "I think I'm coming down with the Flu again". That is exactly what will happen. We issue a "negative permit", and provide fertile mental soil for growth.

We use these types of killer-phrases far too frequently. We fail to realize the consequences of that which we speak. *We are the creators of our own reality.*

"What we *have* is what we *say.* What do we have? What we are saying!" (Charles Capps—*The Tongue*).

One does not have to go far to observe negative attitudes and views on life. How many times a day do we hear people who need something, start their request with: "You don't have etc." Or, "You won't have time to etc."

These spoken phrases are the seeds of defeat. We can all list dozens of everyday things we say that bring us into bondage. We hold ourselves in bondage, [slavery]. *Why?* The problem is that our tongues are *not* under our conscious control.

We know that authentic Christians walking by faith operate from the *spirit.* They do not yield to negative evidence, or to situations with which they are confronted. They do *not* dwell on the problems. In *faith,* they envision the *fruition* of their prayer requests through God's power.

Peter Drucker, has authored many books on managing corporations in which he has stated: "Starve your problems, feed your opportunities." When we experience situations, regardless of their severity, it is human to consistently dwell on the problem. We give it our whole attention. We focus on it. We feed it. It sucks our energy. The more we concentrate on it, the worse it gets! It is *we* who are empowering the problem! We have to disconnect the power-source which is *us!* What a nice introduction to "self-discipline", for truly this is what it is all about!

When authentic Christians move to manage problems, they shift their inner focus. They pray to our heavenly Father for solutions to their problems, in the name of Jesus. It is imperative that the focus be on the desired end result of the prayer requests. It has to come through the Holy Spirit. Yes, this is very difficult, especially when one is hurting, frightened, or desperate. This will always cause us to involuntarily focus on the problem. It will require practiced spiritual wisdom to stay on track.

Even an authentic Christian patient in the Emergency Room has difficulty in concentrating on his prayer. He is surrounded by doctors, bustling nurses, needles and strange sounding equipment, and well may he ask: "How can I focus on health, while I am filled with pain and fear of the unknown?"

This is a typical real life situation, and a tough one to confront. We feel stabs of fear, which brings Satan on the scene. As "Children of Light" we must focus on *faith* to bring God on the scene. We then need to ask: "From where does this alien power originate, that is attempting to possess me, and to exalt itself above God?"

Our failing physical or mental self is still under our control. We are from *below,* God is from *above.* God's Spiritual law will prevail. We are the chosen, ordained sons of God. We have the authority and ability in our prayer requests, to change any situation in which we find ourselves.

The author fully acknowledges his own struggles and failures in this area. He has also experienced success. There is a world of difference between yielding to an alien power, and relaxing in the power of the Spirit, to face a negative physical reality. It all comes down to our current relationship with God, through our Lord Jesus Christ.

Before we arrived at this stage of dire need, had we not established a firm foundation with our heavenly Father? Or, more typically, are we only just now being driven to it by a personal disaster or tragedy of some type?

Is it that we attempt to use God as a "spare-tire" only? Surely, God should be the steering wheel, not the spare-tire! Do we have to be driven to establishing our life-lines? It appears that we do!

Let us reiterate: We do not pray about the problem. God is fully aware of it already. Focussing on the problem is not the solution. Our prayers need to focus on the desired end result of those prayers. (Note the sowing and reaping with the tongue).

We need to monitor our prayers. This whole business of praying and receiving correctly, is something we were never taught. We allowed our pastors to assume that we knew how to pray, when we really did not know. On the other hand; *has any pastor ever asked any one of us at any time, if we knew how to pray?* Or taught us how to pray effectively? We suspect the answer is a resounding: "No!" It's up to us.

"Steven, why are you looking somewhat put-out, or sort of offended"?

"Like ... like ... you really comin' down hard like on them pastors like ..."

"Not really Steven. There are times when *objective judgement* through the Holy Spirit is called for. Pastors, like us, are quite human and equally fallible. We both have common grounds, wherein at times, we struggle with our ability to be 'in the Spirit'. Sometimes pastors surely must wish we had not placed them so high above ourselves in spiritual matters."

Let us re-focus on the matter of praying to our heavenly Father. We need to examine our petitions for their effectiveness. *Steadfast faith is the foundation of prayer.* We are to: "Hold fast the confession of our hope without wavering, for He who promised *is* faithful." (Hebrews 10:23).

Just what did Jesus promise?

"For assuredly, I say to you, whoever says to this mountain, 'Be you removed, and be cast into the sea, and does not doubt in his heart, but believes those things he says will be done, he will have whatever he says. Therefore I say to you, whatever things you ask when you pray, believe that you receive *them*, and you will have *them'*." (Mark 11:23).

The power of prayer is in believing what the Word says. We pray for the mountain, [problem], to be removed. *We see it removed.* We do not yield to the earthly appearances of the situation; otherwise we allow the problem to recur. To that which we yield, its servants we are. (Bondage).

Authentic Christians envision only the *results,* or *fruit* of their prayers. "But let him ask in faith, with no doubting, for he who doubts is like a wave of the sea driven and tossed by the wind. For let not that man suppose that he will receive anything from the Lord, he is a double-minded man, unstable in all his ways." (James 1:6).

Effective prayer ensures that the problem no longer exists. However, we may have to give our prayer time to germinate. Results may not be instantaneous. Time elements are often involved. Some sick people do not wish to be healed. Others block healing by absence of faith. They may be victims of sheer disbelief. In His own home town, Jesus could do little healing.

Steven interjected with: "You mean, the locals thought, He don't know nothin' anyways, He's only the carpenter's son."

"Right", said I.

Healing is a two-way affair. Jesus asked of one person: "What would you have me do?" He had to ascertain the degree of belief, faith and acceptance in that person to ensure that healing could take place.

When authentic Christians pray, they do not hang around for proof that their request has been answered. This would be negating the power of God, by abdicating the throne of Faith. Unconsciously, they would have replaced it with the throne of self.

In praying for others, under the guidance of the Holy Spirit in faith and obedience, the results attained are not our responsibility or problem. We prayed under Holy instructions. We thanked our heavenly Father, and then left the matter in His hands. We thanked Him because the request was fulfilled. Faith-assurance confirmed this. Our self-image has no connection with the result of our prayer request. *We do not exist in this situation, only God does.* That's it! We leave it alone. It is done! We go on our way. Our Father has been glorified.

Let us be fully aware that the results of prayer requests are subject to the degree of faith Christians have in God.

If Christians have weak or non-existent faith, little can be achieved. Success would be automatically negated. Jesus gifted us the operating principles. We have yet to learn how to use them effectively. This is not attempted manipulation of our heavenly Father. It is simply following His instructions.

Most Christians pray without expectation of receiving; other than in a vague manner based on past negative experience. It is as though a prayer request were submitted, and then thrown to the winds; the gods of chance. It is prayer with crossed fingers. It cannot be said that righteousness or intent was absent, only that error in spiritual continuity and connection with God was lacking.

Are we not saying here that most Christians currently need instruction on how to pray effectively? We perceive millions of prayers spoken into the four winds with genuine intent; but the God-linkage is missing. So are the results.

In some churches, upon occasion, the pastor may ask the congregation to pray one-on-one, with the person next to him. As I turn to follow the pastor's instructions, I realize that I do not know this perfect stranger. As I meet his eyes, I may be distracted by a number of factors. More important by far, is the fact that I do not have a God-connection. That which I have been requested to do, creates an immediate impasse, a predicament affording no obvious escape. I may speak a lot of nice Christian words, but I'm broadcasting my prayer seeds into the impotency of nothingness.

Authentic prayer, other than an emergency request of God, takes a little quiet preparation. Prayer is speaking *with* God; it does not comprise careless or casual thoughts and words.

For prayer to be effective, we reiterate, we do not allow appearances to affect us. It may be a matter of health, finances or relationships. We are not moved by fear or any negative factors. Appearances are the *natural-man* problems we were confronting.

Nor do we add an ego-trip-tag at the end of our prayer such as: "If it be Thy will Father." This is a face-saving ego-protection device to excuse us in the eyes of others in event that a miracle did not immediately occur. It negates the power of the prayer and undermines faith as we know it. It is an ugly cop-out. With genuine prayer, we thanked our heavenly Father at the conclusion of our prayer-request, for in faith, we had already received.

When was the last time that we sowed carrot seeds one day, and then poked around in a couple of days to see if they had sprouted? We did not, because even here in the garden, we unconsciously used an elementary form of faith. The same goes for wounds in our bodies, we do not question that healing will take place. It leaves our minds. It is done.

The petitions and prayers of authentic Christians are immersed in the *Now-Faith* of receiving and thanking. "Thank you", is an adjunct simultaneous with receiving. The spoken word of faith, whether in prayer or command of a situation, *"IS"*. Let us be reminded of Proverbs 18:21: "Death and life are in the power of the tongue." Faith is the key.

We are in no way employing the word faith here as in relation to a set of Christian beliefs involving a church, such as Lutheran faith, Seventh Day Adventist, or Catholic faith. This would also include the oft-proclaimed phrase, "His 'faith' brought him through."

The word "faith" in that context, has nothing remotely to do with the faith to which we are referring; which is the miraculous "moving of mountains" faith, gifted us through our heavenly Father.

The New Testament in Hebrews gives us well-defined descriptions of the faith of which we speak.

"Now faith is the substance of things hoped for, the evidence of things not seen. For by it the elders obtained a *good* testimony. By faith we understand that the worlds were framed by the word of God, so that things which are seen were not made of things which are visible." (Hebrews 11:1).

They were created out of thought and the spoken word, and were not made out of existing substances. Note also the words substance and evidence, both of which are solid words with powerful meaning. They are not wishy-washy phantom terms.

"But without faith *it is* impossible to please *Him,* for he who comes to God must believe that He is, and *that* He is a rewarder of those who diligently seek him." (Hebrews 11:6).

For now, we are redefining the term "faith". We will be referring to it as *"Now-Faith"* to capture the core-essence of the type of Faith we are exploring. It is live, active, and result-oriented. It is powerfully demonstrative of Jesus' faith to move mountains.

Now-Faith is Now. Not in the future like "hope". Let us recognize that hope is always about the future. It is our now-action and "Thank You," that releases the power of God! It is a live, conscious act of absolute trust.

St. Augustine said: "Faith is to believe what you do not see; the reward of this faith is to see what you believe."

Authentic Christians will recognize that in activating our *Now-Faith*, there is a "shift-point" that we describe as a pivotal-shift of consciousness, awareness or position. It occurs within our belief system. It is imperative to be conscious of this pivotal-shift if our prayer requests are to be effective.

We have to recognize, that a specific reflex action is required, to pivot or convert Belief into *Now-Faith*. Reflex, because it is not a thinking process, it is God-consciousness. We address the problem or issue at hand. We then humbly yield our prayer request in absolute trust, to our Heavenly Father, in the name of Jesus.

At this point, our prayer circumstance is no longer connected to us. It has been released to our heavenly Father. If we discover we are still connected to the situation, it would indicate that our self is still in charge. This would have negated the pivotal-shift to God, and our entire prayer.

We focus only on the output-objective or end result of our request. We do not focus on, or yield to the circumstances we are confronting. This is a prayer request to God, in the name of Jesus, about a form of change, initiated through us by the Holy Spirit.

At this point our sense of ego and self no longer exist. God fully enters, and acts from within the temple of the Holy Spirit. We are that Temple. It is the Father within who doeth the works. Not "I".

At the apex of our prayer, we become conscious of the pivotal-shift, where Belief pivots into *Now-Faith*. We act. We speak our command to address the situation. This *act* of yielding to the Spirit of God in absolute trust brings our prayer request to fruition.

Man is no longer "here". God is in control. Simultaneously, Man may see that "time" is not, and has become *"Now"*, the spiritual realm of God. Faith and eternity converge to confirm that all things are already complete.

This is an occurrence which within our normal human thinking would be classed as a miracle. Our entire prayer is encompassed in trust. The infallibility of Jesus' Word is our guarantee. The scriptures cannot be broken. When this is accepted, we are immersed in total child-like trust.

"When miracles occur, Man's loss of 'self' has transpired. It is a 'unity of being' suddenly established by which God and the spirit of Man become as one." (From the Lost Notebooks of Wiser-Mouse).

In the process of prayer attainment, authentic Christians are not saying they are God. When the fruit of Now-Faith is being brought forth by the spoken word, we are saying it is an act of co-creation for which man was designed.

It was always appointed to us, as spirit-led sons of God, to "bring things into being", as co-creators with God. Let us confirm the definition of that word "co-create". It means, with, together, jointly, associated in action with another, usually having a lesser share in duty or responsibility.

Co-creation is not equality with God. As individuals we have a body, known as the temple of the Holy Spirit, which we share with the Holy Spirit as He acts through us on instructions from the Father.

Authentic Christians simply obey instructions when they become conscious of prompting by the Holy Spirit. They are not conscious of "self". They are "in the Spirit". This is not an earthly dimension. It is an ethereal bridge between two simultaneous realities.

We are created in God's image and likeness. It is doubtful indeed, that "bringing things into being" would have been excluded from our creation. The Bible proves otherwise. We co-create as a lesser power, under the direction of the Holy Spirit.

We need to reinforce our understanding of Belief and Faith. These are two powerful concepts. We need to fully comprehend them. They are two sides of the same coin, but they are not the same, and not simultaneous. There is a gap between them.

Many Christians have heard a now-fabled story of how a young fellow walked a high-wire rope over Niagara Falls. There are no safety nets and the loud roar of the water is unsettling. Hundreds of spectators are assembled to watch this feat. He addresses the crowd. He smiles. "You *believe* I can do this?" he asks the crowd. "Yes! Yes!" they shout, confirming their *belief.* He does his act. They roar their approval.

Next, he's going to push a wheelbarrow over and back on the high-wire. "You *believe* this can be done too?" he shouts. "Yes!" They give a resounding applaud of *belief* as they urge him on.

He does it. Next he invites a friend to sit in the wheelbarrow on the same high-wire trip. "Do you believe I can do this too?" he challenges. The crowd is beside itself with excitement and approval. "Yes! We *believe* you!" they cry. Once again he does it, and successfully returns. His friend then gets out of the wheelbarrow and climbs down to ground level. "Now", says this faith-filled high-wire artist: "Who's next?"

A great silence fell upon the crowd. No one came forward. Personal *belief* was okay, so long as they were not involved or committed to action. So belief stayed at belief, and nothing more.

The artists on the high-wire had *Now-Faith*. Apparently no one in the vast crowd had high enough personal spiritual power, to trigger the required pivotal-shift from belief into *Now-Faith*.

There must also be a similar pivotal-shift point in bungee jumping, naked or otherwise! The point where belief translates into *Now-Faith* must take over as he jumps. If he's pushed off the launching ramp with belief only, he'll probably scream out in terror. Or, if he is a Christian, yell "Lord! Save me!" We jest, but we admire the enormous courage of those who commit themselves to this act!

The release of *Now-Faith* is an act of commitment. It is a supreme act of trust. When activated, it enables our gifted spiritual creative power to go far beyond mere belief. We become as one with God. He gifts our requests. Our *Now-Faith* forms a definite unity of being with the Holy Spirit. Our forces are now concentrated. They are no longer scattered and blowing like leaves in the wind.

Hope is not belief. Hope is always future-oriented. It has *not* happened yet! Hope says: "I shall receive". This is stage one, wherein it is possible for hope to finally become belief. This is a fact that needs to be spiritually recognized.

Belief is not faith. Belief is always *passive* until it is *activated*, at which time it becomes *Now-Faith*. Peter had to climb out of the fishing boat before he could walk to Christ on the water. The action of getting out, is what pivoted belief into faith. Trust is the lever. It has happened! Faith says: "I have received."

Belief and Faith are almost simultaneous in Jesus' examples. In our "frame by frame" analysis we identify that belief and faith are separate but sequential. In Jesus' works, the pivotal-shift from belief to faith appears to be a combined whole, but *Now-Faith* had to be already present in the recipient.

To reiterate, during this act of *Now-Faith*, we are not "here". We are not personally involved in any connecting sense of self. We have totally abdicated the throne of self.

"Authority cannot be established in the universe without obedience, since authority cannot exist alone." (From the Lost Notebooks of Wiser-Mouse).

Now-faith in action is the engrafted trust gifted us by our heavenly Father. Truly, this is the authentic Christian's cutting-edge of reality!

We all remember when Jesus was entering Capernaum, there came to him a centurion, beseeching him saying: "Lord, my servant lies at home paralyzed, dreadfully tormented." And Jesus said to him, "I will come and heal him."

"The centurion answered and said, 'Lord, I am not worthy that You should come under my roof. But only speak a word, and my servant will be healed. For I also am a man under authority, having soldiers under me. And I say to this *one*, Go, and he goes; and to another, Come, and he comes; and to my servant, Do this, and he does it'."

"When Jesus heard *it*, he marvelled, and said to those who followed, 'Assuredly, I say to you, I have not found such great faith, not in all Israel!'" (Matthew 8:5-10).

"Then Jesus said to the centurion, Go your way, and as you have believed, so be it unto you. And his servant was healed in the self-same hour." (Matthew 8:13). The centurion obeyed his highest power, as did every level below him. The degree of the centurion's unquestioned obedience was ultimate and automatic.

His *pivotal-shift* action was: *"Just speak the word only!"* *Now-Faith* was an everyday occurrence to him. There could be no other! He used his appointed authority. *He,* and *it,* had power.

The centurion recognized and yielded to Christ's authority. So why can't we? For are we not under the same authority? Yes! But one would never know it. We are empowered through the Holy Spirit under the authority of God. One cannot get higher than that. Fallible authorities are not involved at any level. Neither are any man-made church organizations. We need to face facts. Do we take God seriously? Are we committed?

Let us absorb the fact that intent, authority, and obedience, are linked as closely as are the Holy Trinity.

"Empowerment of spiritual authority is released directly in proportion to Man's attained degree of obedience to God's Word. Encompassed by God's authority, it generates the faith-power to achieve miracles." (From the Lost Notebooks of Wiser-Mouse).

That which is below, must obey that which is above or higher. This fact has long been known and may not be fully understood. Individually, as was previously noted, we humans are Spirit, Soul, and Body. Our spirit, [our highest part], is our direct linkage to our heavenly Father through Christ Jesus.

In living God's will, we are in the spirit, and obey the spirit of God. God's plans for us are communicated to us by the Holy Spirit. In turn, our spirit brings the soul into subjection.

The soul is then empowered to control the body. The soul is a higher power than the body. When this linkage is effective we have control over our bodies. This pertains to all matters relating to our health and well-being.

Just being nice and acting in a Holy manner, does not bring us to the cutting-edge of Christian-reality. Jesus said: "These people draw close to Me with their mouth, And honour me with their lips, but their heart is far from Me. And in vain they worship Me, Teaching as doctrines the commandments of men." (Matthew 15:8-9).

Authentic Christians are ambassadors for Christ. We cannot go higher. There is no power greater. We have seen that our words in *Now-Faith* can change circumstances, or move mountains.

So what is holding us back? Why do we allow evil forces of unbelief to entrap us? Is this how we eventually succumb to becoming pseudo-Christians? To that which we yield, its servants we are!

We need to give this very serious thought. Our eternal lives are on the line. What are we going to do about it? It is high time that we broke out from under the domination of: "Having a form of godliness and denying its power." (2 Timothy 3:5).

Many Christians, under the cloud of unbelief, may retreat into a grey, dismal world of their own making. They will also seek out others in order to share their hurtful, negative misery. Yes! Misery does indeed love company.

Personal disaster is created by runaway negative tongues. For some reason, this type of dialogue makes all involved feel rather good! After a grief-confessional session about errant husbands, wives, sex, finances, bodily pains, and malfunctions, the participants go their way.

They feel powerless to break the chains of slavery to evil forces. We always have a choice, but we have to take the first step. How refreshing and life-saving the words of Jesus are: "Come unto me all you who are heavy laden and I will refresh you."

Jesus controlled the weather too! On one occasion the disciples' boat was caught in a great storm at sea, and the disciples awoke Jesus saying:

"'Lord, save us! We are perishing!' But He said to them, 'Why are you fearful, O you of little faith?' Then He arose, and rebuked the winds and the sea; and there was a great calm." (Matthew 8:25-26).

Jesus also marvelled in different ways! In Matthew 8:1, He marvelled at *belief*. Then in Mark 6:6, He marvelled because of their *unbelief*. (To "marvel", is to react with astonishment or intense surprise).

This too, should give us pause for serious thought. If we track Jesus' reasons for marvelling, we get a good wide-angle view of what He saw. We should be "dumbstruck", [made silent by astonishment], by observing how deviant we are from Jesus' viewpoint.

Adam must have been equipped with Now-Faith on automatic pilot, to handle the massive gardening project assigned to him at creation. "Then God said, Let us make man in Our own image, according to Our likeness." (Genesis 1:26).

We too, were imparted with these God-given powers at our creation. By acting on them, the fruit [results] of our *Now-Faith* should be normal everyday occurrences. Not classed as the miracles they appear to be!

You will recall that we lost that power in Eden, when the serpent dropped by for a chat. But we have now regained these powers through our Lord Jesus Christ. When the beguiling serpent showed up, sort of right out of nowhere like snakes do, some dramatic things happened that affected the course and entire content of history.

That brief encounter between Adam and the serpent was far worse for Adam, than being squished in the powerful coils of an anaconda. Far worse, because the very subtlety of the snake's deadly, painless enchantment had the hypnotic power of reasonability.

To this day, we are deeply touched by that meeting of destiny. For it was at that critical point, we became self-conscious, self-reliant and ego-driven. The God-formed clay, had the appalling audacity to question the wisdom of its Maker! Thus it was in Eden, that God first introduced us to the concepts of obedience and authority.

God gave dominion to Adam over every living thing that moves on the earth. In effect, Adam was given complete authority, but was under the rule of obedience to God. When we read the entire record in Genesis, we will find that the serpent, [Satan], lied to Adam in relation to a certain tree in the garden. When Adam acquiesced to the serpent's instructions, he actually committed high treason against God. [Treason: act of handing over; betrayal of a trust]. In other words, Adam sold out to Satan.

Jesus reclaimed the power that Adam relinquished, when He gave His life for us on the cross. We need to experience that which Christ taught. We also may yet need to be *born again* in the spirit. Our failure to commit to this spiritual law; may be the reason that we gather in clumps like turkeys awaiting slaughter.

Returning again to the teachings of Jesus, we come to a case where the disciples could not cast out an evil spirit from a certain man's son. The father of the demon-possessed son said: "So I spoke to Your disciples, that they should cast it out, but they could not." "Jesus answered him and said, 'O faithless generation, how long shall I be with you? How long shall I suffer for you? Bring him to me'." (Mark 9:18).

"Jesus said to him, 'If you can believe, all things *are* possible to him who believes'. Immediately the father of the child cried out and said with tears, 'Lord, I believe; help my unbelief!'" (Mark 9:23).

It is imperative for us to understand Jesus' explanation of why the disciples had failed to cast out this demon.

"And when He had come into the house, His disciples asked Him privately, 'Why could we not cast it out?'. So He said to them, 'This kind can come out by nothing but prayer and fasting'."

Spiritual belief is that which enables the birth of faith. It is both sequential, and simultaneous. In "time", Man experiences gaps in continuity of process-flow. In *Now,* he lives in simultaneity, he is complete.

Note that the technical term "simultaneity" is never quite accurate. Simultaneity has micro-flow-motion of which we are not cognizant.

Here's another interesting case wherein Jesus was on his way to heal a young girl. Crowds surrounded him. "Now a woman, having a flow of blood for twelve years, who had spent all her livelihood on physicians, and could not be healed by any, came from behind and touched the border of His garment. And immediately her flow of blood stopped. And Jesus said, 'Who touched Me?'" (Luke 8:43-45).

46. "But Jesus said, 'Somebody has touched me, for I perceived power going out from Me'." [The woman confessed it was her]. 48. "And he said to her, 'Daughter, be of good cheer, your faith has made you well. Go in peace'."

Here we see that the *belief* that people had, was translated into *Now-Faith* by the *act* of touching Jesus' garment. *[The act was the pivotal-shift].* "And begged Him that they might only touch the hem of His garment. And as many as touched *it* were made perfectly well." (Matthew 14:36).

Let us be aware that these were ordinary folk who needed healing for some ailment. They were not sophisticated, educated, or even religious types. Probably most were peasants. For the first time, they used Christian principles even as they were being demonstrated by Jesus.

No study of faith-in-action would be complete without further analyzing how we can walk on water! We find the disciples in a boat, being tossed around in the sea with a high wind in the fourth watch of the night. It is here we find Jesus coming to them by walking on the sea!

"And when the disciples saw him walking on the sea, they were troubled, saying, 'It is a ghost!' And they cried out with fear." (Matthew 14:26).

"But immediately Jesus spoke to them, saying, 'Be of good cheer! It is I; be not afraid'. And Peter answered him and said, 'Lord, if it is You, command me to come to You on the water'. So He said 'Come.' And when Peter had come down out of the boat, he walked on the water to go to Jesus." (Matthew 14:27-29).

Note the pivotal-shift from belief to Now-Faith, triggered by the act of leaving the boat.

"But when he saw the wind *was* boisterous, he was afraid; and beginning to sink he cried out, saying, 'Lord, save me!'.

And immediately Jesus stretched out His hand, and caught him, and said to him, 'O you of little faith, why did you doubt?' And when they got into the boat, the wind ceased." (Matthew 14:30-32).

Observe that as soon as Peter reverted to *natural-soul-man*, and became self-centred in his body, he began to sink. Peter failed to maintain his faith in the Spirit.

Here is another powerful and beautiful example of *Now-Faith* in action. It is the piece-de-resistance of what we call sheer spiritual elegance!

Jesus is coming to see Lazarus, brother of Martha and Mary, having received word that Lazarus was sick. "When Jesus heard *that*, He said, 'This sickness is not unto death, but for the glory of God, that the Son of God may be glorified through it'." (John 11:4).

"Our friend Lazarus sleeps, but I go that I may wake him up. However, Jesus spoke of his death, but they thought that He was speaking about taking rest in sleep. Then said Jesus to them plainly, 'Lazarus is dead'." (John 11:11-13).

Upon arriving at the grave: "They took away the stone *from the place* where the man was lying. And Jesus lifted up *His* eyes and said, 'Father, I thank You that You have heard Me. And I know that You always hear Me, but because of the people who are standing by I said *this,* that they may believe that You sent Me.' Now when He had said these things, He cried with a loud voice, 'Lazarus, come forth!' And he who had died came out."

The greatest prayer of which man is capable is: "Thank you Father". In faith, the prayer petition has already been granted. [It was complete before it started!]. We need to study this stunning "faith-sequence". It is rarely enlarged upon, and escapes the attention or emphasis of those who speak on it.

Jesus did *not* say: "Lazarus come forth" and then say, "Thank you Father." It was the other way round. First, came: "Thank you Father". [*pivotal-shift*], and secondly, came the already granted prayer petition. The command was "Come forth!"

"Thank you Father", simply confirms that it was already done. Why would one give thanks for that which has not been received? (This miracle was pure Godly *Now-Faith* in action).

We reiterate, that point where *Belief* translates into *Faith* is the *pivotal-shift-point.* The decision to *act* occurs in consciousness, resulting directly from spiritual authority born out of our engrafted trust in God.

"Authority is established to execute God's order. Man is a steward of this authority. As such, he represents God in his every word and action." (From the Lost Notebooks of Wiser-Mouse).

There are many more pivotal-shifts to be observed such as: "Cast your nets", or, "Go wash in the pool". The act of casting and the act of washing were the triggering pivotal-shift points. These were attained by adopting a child-like trust. These acts of obedience in trust were *Now-Faith* in action.

Allow me to parallel the fabled high-wire act above Niagara Falls at a more personal level. It is a glorious summer day, and quite late in the afternoon. We are in the Kananaskis region of Southern Alberta. It is true wilderness. My wife and our three boys aged about seven, five and two years old, were on a short wilderness trip to see some beaver kits I had previously discovered.

On the way to the beaver ponds, we waded across a shallow creek some forty feet wide. We walked in the hot sun, accompanied by our miniature Dachshund "Pepi", for some two and a half miles. After spending a restful couple of hours watching the beavers, it was time to return to our vehicle.

As we approached our crossing point, I became alarmed at the loud roar of fast water. We stopped at the creek edge, and were dismayed to see about three to four feet of water swiftly broiling by.

The power company far up-stream had opened the gates on its dam to reduce water pressure. Twilight was descending. By this time the sun was red and very low in the western sky. What do we do? Here we are with three very tired, hot and hungry kids, my wife and the dog.

We are far off any highway, and deep into bear country with both blacks and grizzlies on the evening prowl. Not a good outlook! This is a prime example of that which turns nature lovers, from "observers", into "prey".

We scanned an old deserted broken-down logging road bridge just a little way up from our original crossing. Among the remaining rotted and broken logs, only one fairly solid seventy foot log remained to span the creek.

If we did not cross on it, we would have to walk about six miles to get across the creek by a regular bridge, and then the same six miles back to our vehicle, a total of twelve miles by starlight. This is a disastrous scenario of the first magnitude. So this is *"it?"* Oh! No! Oh! Yes! There is no other way!

I'm somewhat unsettled by heights, especially when one false step would mean falling into the swift current with results we do not want to contemplate. In hiking boots, putting one foot before the other, I triggered the first of three pivotal-shift prayer journeys in *Now-Faith,* by carrying our dog "Pepi" across. I made it.

Now, I have to return on that same single seventy foot log, that's crossing number two! This was achieved. Next my wife and the two older boys had to cross. They "humped" their way over by straddling the log.

All was well, except for the youngest boy, who was so small he could not straddle the crossing. I mounted him on my shoulders, instructing him not to let go at any time, under any circumstance.

He was fully aware that if we fell we would be swept downstream for quite a way, but we would make it. So I instructed him to grimly hold on, regardless of what might occur.

This would be my third pivotal-shift point of action in *Now-Faith* of the day. It is action, triggered by need of, and *trust* in my heavenly Father. Before I step onto the log of destiny I again say: "Thank You Father", in deep humility. "Thank you", because the journey is already a completed act before I take my first step! I only envision us safely joining the rest of the family. I step on the log for the final crossing with my precious cargo. My mission is complete.

I so clearly recall those three pivotal-shifts from *Belief,* to *seventy feet of Now-Faith.* One walks between two worlds by primarily being in the spiritual one. One must never yield power to unforgiving circumstances; the roar of the fast water, the possibility of a single foot slipping, or of drowning and losing myself and my youngest son. It is emotional to write of this even after so many years. Thank You Father.

There are many documented cases of Jesus teaching us how to access and use our God-gifted powers. We must be alert to the fact that most of we Christians have a form of godliness, but deny its power!

In Matthew 6:31 we read: "Therefore do not worry, saying, 'What shall we eat?' or 'What shall we drink?' or 'What shall we wear?' For your heavenly Father knows that you need all these things."

What do we make of this? For a start, these days most people in our Western culture have never really needed anything. Few of us have ever had to fast for four or five days at a time due to lack of money, credit cards, friends, or government resources.

In most cases, we've had an adequate education, at the very least high school. When did we ever have to rely on God to provide for us in the way the Bible portrays?

Those who have been gifted a commission-paying position in sales, know only too well that one performs positively, or one has no job. They are paid for results achieved. There are no hand-outs or excuses for lack of effective performance. One does not have a salaried position along with an attitude of entitlement. This is a challenging combination for achievement and for personal growth.

Let us now examine a few verses of scripture on the matter of believing, and mixing the term belief in with faith. Many Christians proclaim that, "They are one and the same thing". Some say: "Yes, I believe", but have no evidence of their "faith". However, in James 1:22 we are instructed: "But be doers of the word, and not just hearers only, deceiving yourselves."

We need to take another look at James 2:14: "What *does* it profit, my brethren, if someone says he has faith but does not have works? Can faith save him?"

In today's vernacular, James is saying: "Okay wise guy, put your money where your mouth is." We Christians talk about belief and faith, but what results of faith have we ever achieved? When have we ever had to "Trust in the Lord with all our heart"? Have we been granted our prayer requests in faith for food and garments? Or for our transportation, be it by car, boat, donkey or camel?

Now James, what's next? James 2:17: "Thus also faith by itself, if it does not have works, is dead. 18: But someone will say, 'You have faith, and I have works. Show me your faith without your works, and I will show you my faith by my works'.

Even so faith, if it has no works, is dead, being alone. 19: You believe that there is one God. You do well. Even the demons believe, and tremble! 20: But do you want to know, O foolish man, that faith without works is dead?"

Maybe we Christians have to re-evaluate our basic understanding of what belief and faith are all about. If we have *Now-Faith,* the evidence of that faith will be apparent.

Trusting in God is the key for all authentic Christians, and a simple prayer to activate *Now-Faith* in any situation is found in Proverbs 3:5: "Trust in the Lord with all your heart, And lean not to your own understanding; 6: In all your ways acknowledge Him, and He shall direct your paths." Note:

"All our ways". We cannot hold anything back as in: "OK Lord, you can run things, but don't interfere with finances or sex. I'll take care of those. You do your part, and I'll do mine!" What?

In this prayer, we are simply yielding to the guidance of the Holy Spirit. Again, acting in complete trust, knowing that we shall be obedient to the instructions we receive. There is no stress in trust and obedience, even when one's actions and plans are changed and appear to be devoid of logic!

Here is where we run into our failure to know how to think correctly. Our educational systems have never taught us how to effectively use our minds in the way they were designed to perform. [It is truly a case of the blind leading the blind]. Generally, right-brained intuitive awareness is not consciously acknowledged, or actively monitored in our everyday mental processes.

It even appears to be locked out. Intuition is not of main-stream recognition. It is an undeveloped element which we only occasionally encounter. We need to harness this power with ever-increasing frequency.

When we are commanded to: "Lean not to your own understanding", this means, do not use logic only. Logic is merely the science of the formal principles of reasoning. It is reliant upon "left-brain" thinking only. We do not deride logic-based thinking; we could not live without it. We should be questioning why we make no conscious effort to apply intuitive thinking to our everyday lives. We need this "whole-brain" approach.

From the fountain of the interior life in man, springs this mysterious power to see and feel the truth. It is called *intuition*. It is the power to instantly perceive, to *see* and to *know*. It is spiritual perception, and not connected to logic.

"Intuitive thinking expands Man's thought processes exponentially. It extends far beyond logic. It originates in 'Now', and is spiritual in nature." (From the Lost Notebooks of Wiser-Mouse).

Intuitive thinking, and spiritual perception, are both right-brain concepts. All spiritual matters including the scriptures; and the concepts of being born again, as well as *Now-Man*, and *Now-Faith*, are right-brain functions only. They belong in the world of *"All-Power"*.

Developing right-brained spiritual awareness; and ascending to higher levels of consciousness is the recurring theme of the Bible. It's what the Bible is all about! We are not yet complete! We have been gifted a body, and logical mind. However, it is up to *us* to develop ourselves further, for our flight-path to eternity. We have to do it! It is not an assumed entitlement.

As we know, the left-brain is the logical half, which is directly linked to natural or Time-man. It is primarily focussed on those matters within its sphere; namely, the body and worldly molecular elements. This represents the average human being.

Power in left-brained thinking, is conceptualized as force, a power to control or change. It originates in self, and unwittingly supplants God. It resides in the Time-realm with Time-man. This concept of left-brain logic-force is alien to *Now-Man*.

Now-Man's *"All-Power"*, on the other hand, [from Time-man's viewpoint], is actually *no* power! *"All-power"* resides in *Now*, and is therefore not accessible to Time-man.

Now-Man, being a son of God, does not require "left-brained power, originating in logic." His God-gifted authority and power, is hidden within humility and obedience. He operates in *Now-Faith*, under the full power of God's Word. He is subject to, and is a part of "I AM". "I AM", is all-power. It does not have to announce its presence. It "IS".

Intuitive thinking will relay to us flashes of insight which may bring an immediate change of plan or action. It is directly connected with immediate obedience. One can resist, but if we do, we will face the consequences. Only later do we realize that what seemed to be illogical was perfectly correct. The more we experience the effective results of intuitive thinking, the more powerful our correct actions will be. This is the way we were designed! Yes! *Designed*, not evolved!

"What will they think?" is a common excuse for not acting upon intuitive guidance. Do *they* run our lives, whoever they are? It should cause authentic Christians to be filled with compassion and not condemnation. We have to walk in love to assist others' learning curves and growth. For not so long ago, we were in the same position.

It is imperative that we develop this ability of awareness, and to consciously use the intuitive mode of thought. We must habitually monitor our internal reception. Obedience to instructions should be automatic. As logic-only persons, half of us is missing! We are beings that are undeveloped, and psychologically incomplete.

We have powerful latent thinking abilities. However, we do not have to go through life as lame ducks. Even if one leaves Christianity out of it, straight logic only, lacks mental competence. It is *we* who must develop all facets of our right-brain thinking.

We have daily examples of people saying: "I had a hunch", or "I had a gut feeling" about something. This is usually said in an apologetic or rueful manner, to excuse a result he has achieved. This way his ego is not damaged in the face of absolute unbelief. There is body language expressed, to offset the guilt of being an intuitive thinker. He should not have to be defensive.

In the recognition and use of intuitive direction, authentic Christians do not have this internal conflict. If they do, they are not "in the Spirit". Christians acting upon instructions from the Holy Spirit, have immutable power. They image. They listen. They trust. They act. They let go. It is done! They do not empower the problem. The desired output result has already been achieved in *Now-Faith*.

We observe that our churches and Christian gatherings rarely allude to, or place any particular importance on intuitive thinking. This surely should be primary in Christian training, as it involves all spiritual matters. It is an adjunct to receiving messages from our heavenly Father through the Holy Spirit.

We need also to be aware of other powers, satanic in nature, which frequent the intuitive receiving areas of our minds.

In order to receive spiritual guidance from God, we have to sharply focus our awareness. This is a commitment we effect in conjunction with our Gatekeeper.

There are however, many devout Christians who firmly reject what we have stated in our section on Belief and Now-Faith. They say that these concepts are linked to our manipulating God, in order to receive our prayer requests. There is no way in which God can be manipulated.

Their belief is that Christians will be blessed according to the will of God, and in the due course of time their prayers will be answered. In the meantime, we should all "bear our cross". This equates with continued suffering, pain and misery, poor finances, bad health, and stressful personal relationships. These are products of zero-faith.

We apparently have to be grateful for small mercies, if and when they should ever arrive. People keep "a-hopin" and "a-prayin", but nothing happens. This could be called unchristian-fatalism.

There are many changes and healings that could take place, but not through unchristian-fatalism. These Christians go through the acts, motions and procedures, but belief is weak. Faith may be even weaker, or non-existent. Their belief system would appear to be intellectual, and of *natural-soul-based-man*. It has the appearance of pseudo-Christianity.

It would appear that on the basis of this unchristian-fatalism, we are at the mercy of a God who may, or may not, hear our prayers. We are merely hoping, and that is all about a vague future time. Nothing is going to happen unless more scriptural Christian growth occurs.

There also exists in this same camp of criticism, examples of how wrong they believe *Now-Faith* is, by citing some typical examples of alleged error. One case is where a group of young women wanted to cross a river. Filled with belief, they made a prayer request, then stepped boldly into the strong current, and were all swept away and drowned. They erred, not knowing the Scriptures.

Another example is the "taking up of poisonous serpents", based on Paul, when he was making a fire after being ship-wrecked. A venomous snake bit his hand and hung on, that is, until he shook it off into the fire. (Acts 28:5). He was unharmed. In this context we can do likewise? Still another example is consciously eating or drinking poisonous fluids or substances; they shall not hurt us? Or how about deliberately exposing ourselves to a recognized danger? There is nothing scriptural in these beliefs.

Under this unchristian-fatalism concept, there is the inevitable requesting of God for luxurious housing, automobiles, or exotic travel backed by huge bank accounts! These thoughts are based on shallow thinking, devoid of any true spiritual knowledge.

These examples are quite incorrect. This is known as tempting God, which cannot be done, because God does not respond to such ignorance. This is us placing God in a subordinate position, where He has to do our bidding. What? Shall the clay demand of the potter, I want this or that?

These are attempts at gross manipulation based on whimsy or shallow understanding. In some cases, the *intent* was genuine, but vastly misguided. It lacked the spiritual knowledge and authority to act. When we pray in accordance to the will of God, we are confident that our prayers will be answered.

Authentic Christians addressing mountains to be moved, or rivers to be parted, act in mature spiritual knowledge. They then obey the promptings of the Holy Spirit. Authentic Christians will recognize these impartations as the power of God in action.

They will act in *Now-Faith* in absolute obedience and trust. They will not yield to the appearances of a situation. Having prayed, they know they have already received, and immediately, give thanks to our heavenly Father.

Let us now return to the healings of Jesus and *Now-Faith*. We note that Jesus always had compassion for the individual. Just what is compassion?

Do we have it? Have we ever felt it? It must have its roots in empathy which is being aware of, and sensitive to, the feelings, thoughts and experiences of another. We note by Jesus' examples that compassion is an integral part of giving, supporting and healing.

Without this compassionate mind-set, which runs deeply through our Christian psyche, our healing efforts may be negated. It appears that compassion is linked to attaining the "pivotal-shift" points in our prayer requests.

"Finally, all of *you be* of one mind, having compassion for one another; love as brothers, *be* tender-hearted, *be* courteous." (1 Peter 3:8).

Throughout the Scriptures, we are reminded of our mindsets, regardless of our spiritual aspirations and actions. At times, in our humanness, we act in rebellion to the somewhat strict mental discipline required of us. We will not always be in line with the instructions from our Gatekeeper.

A thought-provoking question that applies to all of us is to ask: "Who runs us?" We unconsciously believe that "we" run us, who else? It's a tough one. Is it not true that mostly our bodies and souls run us? We like to believe that we run ourselves, but most of the time that is simply not true!

"No man can escape from himself unless he has 'somewhere to go'. The inner-states of Man undergo gradual spiritual evolution." (From the Lost Notebooks of Wiser-Mouse).

Once again we refer to Paul's famous passage in Romans 7:19: "For the good that I will *to do*, I do not do; but the evil I will not *to do*, that I practice.

20: Now if I do what I will not *to do*, it is no longer I who *do* it, but sin that dwells in me. 21: I find then a law, that evil is present with me, the one who will to do good."

"When Man undertakes to bring his life into relationship with God, he embarks upon a serious and demanding task. There is no leeway for self-deception, dream or illusion". (From the Lost Notebooks of Wiser-Mouse).

With unerring spiritual accuracy the spectre of self-control captures us!

Let's take a peek at Romans 8:5: "For those live according to the flesh set their minds on the things of the flesh, but those *who* live according to the Spirit, the things of the Spirit. 6: For to be carnally minded *is* death, but to be spiritually minded *is* life and peace."

So we've come full circle! Jesus may well ask: "Are you for me, or against Me?" Are we in an in-between state? A city divided against itself must fall. Dare it be mentioned again what happens to tepid Christians? (Jesus: "I will spew you out of My mouth.").

"No man can serve two masters; for either he will hate the one and love the other, or else he will be loyal to the one and despise the other. You cannot serve God and mammon." (Matthew 6:24).

These are all questions we will eventually need to confront, regardless of how defensive we feel. This is the cutting-edge of reality in our lives. Are we going to make excuses, deny, hide, or "space out"? We're talking about eternity here!

It would appear that even authentic Christians still have a lot of catching-up to do. However, now that we know what it is in ourselves that we need to change, we are in a position to do something about it! We've been through some pretty heavy-duty stuff so far, so let's lighten-up with a little God-given humour!

CHAPTER FIVE

Steve and I were out adventuring, and had set up camp at a remote wilderness lake location. It was a perfect summer evening. We had met under similar circumstances as loners several years ago, and had been captured by the beauty and freedom of such wild places.

The camp-fire had burned down to a rich red glow ready for our wiener-roast. The beans were simmering, and in complete opposition to 1 Thessalonians 5:22, to "Abstain from every form of evil", we uncapped two more Heinekens to toast each other and the distant snow-capped mountains.

Steve looked expectantly across at me. Firelight flickered on his finely-chiselled features. Steve is young in his Christian comprehension, and looks to me for both spiritual guidance and adventure. Being some twenty years my junior, typical of his age group, it would be another ten years or so before his primary life focus would slowly migrate northward to his intelligence centre. His Christian journey was not always on track, but he seemed comfortable with my biblical explanations.

Anyway, it was time for a Christian bed-time story. I related the occasion of when our church had a special women's banquet. We were to serve supper to some sixty-five women that evening. There is something about an assignment like this that joyfully possesses me. I become the part completely, with articulate English accent, [natural], slightly bowed head, and subservient attitude.

I added classical acquiescence to their every wish. The pastor said grace, and the hungry guests dutifully bowed their heads in reverent gratitude.

It seemed that never had these harried, pressured mothers and housewives been treated so royally. "Would Madam prefer the steak and tiger prawns, or the salmon with tiger prawns?" The answer to either would of course be: "Excellent choice Madam."

I was gifted with the precious reward of their surprised and grateful expressions. They were so totally unaccustomed to being truly treated as though *each* were a part of the Royal Family.

A buzz went round the tables. I performed so well that I was invited by several ladies to oversee their upcoming parties. The dinner proceeded smoothly, and all was well; *but not quite.* Needing a brief break, I joined a group at a large table at which the pastor's wife convened.

The guests all beamed at me in appreciation. Then it happened. I know not why, but it just spilled out of me, just like a movie unfolding. Eying the giant tiger prawns and picking one up, I gained their attention. Then in my usual highly-animated way of expressing myself, eyeing them and the prawn, I said: "This takes me back to the time when I served at the Royal House of Windsor, under Prince Philip, for some eighteen years at Windsor Castle."

Eyes widened, attentions riveted, I continued, "One night we had one of those relatively informal dinners so-called, even though they were superbly planned. There were the usual dignitaries, including guests from abroad, which on this occasion included Queen Wilhelmina from Holland." There were gasps of surprise, admiration, and wonder at being personally served by Prince Philip's top staff member who had actually served a queen!

Their attention was drilling into me. I swept on: "As I served Queen Wilhelmina, I think I may have been too distracted by her ample bosom because, Oh! No! A giant tiger prawn I was about to place on her plate, flipped from my tongs, and disappeared down her cleavage! Oh! My God!

Simultaneously, I will never forget the expression on Prince Philip's face, his fork half-way to his mouth, he froze, and then he saw me quickly dive my left hand down the Queen's cleavage to retrieve the errant prawn. The queen deeply flushed from her diamond tiara, right down to 'never-never' land. I transferred the prawn to my pocket, and carried on serving, having apologized profusely to that great lady.

At this point, the pastor's wife was as flushed as Queen Wilhelmina as she desperately tried to stop me from saying any more. This was far outside her guests' comfort zone. Come to think of it, the woman on my left looked equally flushed, but that was probably because my eyes were drawn to her equally queenly endowment.

But, I gallantly continued with my story: "Dessert was a decadent chocolate mousse, and as I placed the tall-stemmed crystal glass in front of Queen Wilhelmina, she, she did the unthinkable! [I thought the pastor's wife was going to faint]. With her right hand the queen tweaked my derriere!

It was a hard enough pinch that it became my turn to blush profusely. The queen had a wicked look in her impish eyes. Shortly after, Prince Philip caught my eye, and immediately after dinner, I was banished from Windsor Castle forever! The moral to the story must surely be, that 'bosoms and tiger prawns' should be kept apart!"

Steve screamed with laughter as he almost fell backward off his log. "Like ... you done got your bosoms and prawns all mixed up like!"

"You can say that again! But Steve! There's more! The next day being Sunday, our pastor from the pulpit said: 'We didn't know that we had such a distinguished person in our congregation until yesterday at the banquet. Derek served under Prince Philip for some eighteen years at Windsor Castle, before coming to Canada'. Oh! No! Don't they realize that a lot of what I say is in parentheses? I'll never live this down!"

After more hilarity, Steve cleaned up, and before turning in, we tossed down another couple of Heinekens to complete our evening. A lone wolf howled from somewhere far away in the forest. Bats zapped-up our insect enemies, and slowly the moon rose. The magic of another perfect summer night embraced our camp and the entire valley.

Okay! It's time to get serious again!

So what are we all about? I'm *me,* and you are *you.* We generally know the status of our fleshly bodies. But do we have a clue as where we stand in our spiritual development? What does the Bible say? Let us discover what we are, where we are, and where we need to be on "Graduation Day" as we prefer to call it, you know, when we pass on into eternity.

Being Christians in Christ, we will be resurrected from the dead. It is written in 1 Corinthians 15:35: "But someone will say, How are the dead raised up? And with what body do they come? 36: Foolish one, what you sow is not made alive unless it dies. 37: And what you sow, you do not sow that body that shall be, but mere grain, perhaps wheat or some other grain. 38: But God gives it a body as He pleases, and to each seed its own body."

"The body is sown in corruption, it is raised in incorruption. It is sown in dishonour, it is raised in glory. It is sown in weakness, it is raised in power. It is raised a spiritual body. There is a natural body, and a spiritual body." (1 Corinthians 15:42-44).

"So when this corruptible has put on incorruption, and this mortal has put on immortality, then shall be brought to pass the saying that is written: *'Death is swallowed up in victory. O Death, where is your sting? O Hades, where is your victory?'"* (1 Corinthians 15:54-55).

"Okay Steve! Why the quizzical look?"

"Like ... if I'm gonna get swallowed up like ... by a grizzly ... my death is really a victory for him like ... an' death don't sting like? ... it must hurt like hell to have your skull crushed ..."

"Of course being attacked by a grizzly, or whatever, is a bit different. Fortunately, the brain produces pain killers far more powerful than morphine, so you won't feel pain as such."

"But while we *are* speaking of death, let's check this out. 'And fear not them that kill the body, but are not able to kill the soul: but rather fear him which is able to destroy both soul and body in hell'." (Matthew 10:28).

"Like ... I'll watch out for them bears like ... and for sure the evil one ... he's able to kill the body and the soul like ..." Steven looked disturbed, but he also had that competent look that said he could handle either one.

We have stated before, that our sojourn on earth is relatively short. As we progress further into the Christian life, we learn increasingly to understand that: "For what is highly esteemed among men is an abomination in the sight of God." (Luke 16:15). This means that our value system will be both challenged and changed.

We do not need to doubt that the resurrection of our body is ahead, for the Spirit of resurrection is within us. What is it we need to learn now, that will be so necessary before, and after our departure?

It is to walk by faith, and not by sight! This is the "eternity principle", and we need to learn and practice its laws of operation while here. Being sons of God, and joint heirs with our Lord Jesus Christ, we will also be co-creators in eternity. We too will "bring things into being" by the spoken word.

There is no direct pathway between time and eternity. Remember that Time-man's *now* is on a horizontal line. Our *Now* dimension is vertical to this. Eternity is not an extension of time as we know it. These are different categories of experience. When time ends, eternity begins. We leave time.

Time means that we are locked into a pattern of chronological sequence which we are helpless to break. There really is no past or future. There is only the present moment in time, wherein all events occur. Let us make it count.

"Now" is eternity. *God is Now*. In Him, we live and move and have our being. The kingdom of heaven is also contained in *Now*. When we consciously live in the presence of our heavenly Father; humbly submitting our petitions of Him in the name of Jesus, we are living on earth in the manner that God planned for us.

We learn from the Father that spoken words are life. "So shall My word be that *goes* forth from My mouth; It shall not return to Me void, But it shall accomplish what I please, and it shall prosper *in the thing* for which I sent it." (Isaiah 55:11).

The reality of our situation is that Man has fallen asleep in matter, in time, and in himself. What is man? He is us. He is a series of states of consciousness. A man can only be truly known by his level of consciousness, and his understanding of Time. Our souls are connected with Eternity. They are sown into Time.

Thus we have the Parable of the Sower in the Gospels, a thought-provoking study. Why do we have such difficulty in seeing that we have a future? We need to be reminded of: "O death where is your sting? O grave where is your victory?" Our whole being is designed to have a future.

The illusion of passing-time causes us to fix our eyes on tomorrow, which never comes, for it is always tomorrow! We live ahead of ourselves, and are never here. The key to "being here", is to rise above time. This is where we feel and experience the presence of God. We must come to accept that sometime, somehow, the only place where anything *real* can happen is in "Now".

Our real future lies in our ability to grow in comprehension. To bring about a gradual transformation of ourselves, we need to search the Holy Scriptures with all due diligence, and live the Word of God.

"Time is a graveyard of lost souls. Man only truly dies when he fails to discover, or forgets, why he was born into this parenthesis in Eternity." (From the Lost Notebooks of Wiser-Mouse).

We have previously referred to new levels of consciousness, or dimensions that are contained in *Now.* We experience these as a revelation. It is like seeing the world that we knew with different eyes and powers of perception. This subtle experience of rising above time; is as gentle and as beautiful as dawn breaking on a new day, which it is.

A parallel experience is, "For the kingdom of God *is* not in word but in power." (1 Corinthians 4:20).

Our Lord Jesus spoke about kingdom of God, in Luke 17:20, "Now when he was asked of the Pharisees when the kingdom of God would come, He answered them and said, 'The kingdom of God does not come with observation; 21: nor will they say, 'See here!' or 'See there!' For indeed, the kingdom of God is within you."

God is not "out there". He is here within each of us. So these strikingly powerful events occur within us, as we grow in Christ. They come upon us in due course of chronological time, without any fanfare, and are quite unobtrusive. But their effect is beyond measure.

Another clue is to be seen in Matthew 7:13, which primarily give focus to our life-choices. It reads: "Enter by the narrow gate; for wide *is* the gate and broad *is* the way that leads to destruction, and there are many who go in by it. Because narrow *is* the gate and difficult *is* the way which leads to life, and there are few who find it."

The mainstream of humanity, if they reflect on this concept at all, mistakenly believes that "all roads lead to Rome."

No other religion outside of Christianity, lays claim to the resurrection of the dead. Humanity is primarily glued to its five senses, its bodies, and its souls. Few are they who rise authentically to a spiritual level. We either live unto ourselves, or we make the Lord our habitation. (Are you with Me or against Me?).

Thus far, we have spoken only of those levels of awareness which pertain specifically to authentic Christianity. But there are many who may ask about other levels of awareness or consciousness that they have attained. We will address these with caution.

It is factual to state that these other levels do exist. We should be aware that there are many among us, who have experienced these dimensions quite unwittingly. They just "happened". So what do we make of this?

As Christians, we may be led to explore these revelations and inputs. However, our newly-acquired knowledge must never give rise to increases of ego strength, or of dethroning the *spiritual-man* in favour of the soul-instincts of *natural-man*. Our allegiance still needs to be aligned with the will of God, under instructions from the Holy Spirit. Being "one in the spirit" will largely depend on how obedient we are to our Gatekeeper.

Before going into personal discoveries, here is that Elijah case. This is a wondrous story of Elijah taking a city which is very well defended and heavily armed. In the early light of morning the odds looked insurmountable to Elisha, his young servant. As he surveyed the defences with which they were confronted, he says to Elijah: "Alas, my master! What shall we do?" (2 Kings 6:15).

16: "And he answered, 'Do not fear, for those who are with us *are* more than those who *are* with them.' 17: And Elijah prayed, and said, 'Lord, I pray, open his eyes that he may see'."

"Then the Lord opened the eyes of the young man, and he saw. And behold, the mountain *was* full of horses and chariots of fire all around Elisha." (This is an exciting little adventure wherein we see the results of prayer).

We see from this, that there *are* other levels of insight and veils covering consciousness. Elijah's servant had the privilege of that experience. This is valid because it is scriptural. We need to be aware of the danger in developing interest in exploring other dimensions of consciousness. It may lead us to becoming captive to false satanic insights, wherein lie a wide spectrum of ideas relating to the spirit of error.

New Age doctrines, and a myriad of other teachings from Eastern and Western religions, can be sown deeply within us. We may also be subject to slow seepage of other alien doctrines.

"When Man elects to replace the Word of God with the word of Man, he has become a power unto himself. He has separated his spirit from God's Spirit. In so doing, Man has sown the seeds of his destruction". (From the Lost Notebooks of Wiser-Mouse).

This has a startling similarity to the "tree of knowledge", whereby we, through Adam, now have access to both good and evil. Adam against instructions from God ate of that tree. Genesis 2:17: "For in the day that you eat of it you shall surely die."

That which a person has experienced as revelation beyond that which is biblical; however real to him, may well be the planting of evil seed by the evil one. There is just enough scriptural truth blended with untruth that it may lead him astray. Yes! Curiosity did kill the cat! It has power to destroy us too. The fertile soil of curiosity, the seeking of special knowledge outside of that which God has revealed to us, is adding to the scriptures. We need to read of the dire consequences of such actions. Christian doctrine forbids this. It is an element in the Christian foundational structure of obedience. (Revelation 22:18).

Paul was no stranger to comprehension of higher levels of consciousness. In 1 Corinthians 12:1 he states: "It is doubtless not profitable for me to boast. I will come to visions and revelations of the Lord. 2: I know a man in Christ who fourteen years ago, whether in the body I do not know, God knows, such a one was caught up to the third heaven."

The scriptures refer to three heavens. The first is the sky or firmament, the second is the cosmos with planets, stars, and galaxies. The third heaven is another state of being, where consciousness attains entry to the Presence of God and Eternity.

It is a shared experience for those at Paul's level who rise above "time", to see and hear that which has no meaning or relation to our world. No language can capture the utterances heard in that dimension.

In Revelation, John was also stretched to his limit in explaining what he saw and heard. It was an incredible feat for him to express that which he grasped in mind, and reduce it to words in order to communicate with us. Symbols are often used to encompass vast concepts into single images to enable our comprehension.

World-wide, there are millions of religious people who follow spiritual teachings other than Christianity, including that which is known as "cosmic consciousness". They all worship God, but they follow different truths and cosmic beliefs. Most have their own specific language to portray their particular version of the kingdom of heaven. Usually this is a state of being, well beyond that which linguistics can describe or attain.

In the book entitled *Cosmic Consciousness*, some of the documented great names of those who attained that state, are Gautama the Buddha, Mohammed, William Blake, Walt Whitman, Jacob Boehme, Plotinus, Balzac, and Dante.

Our Lord Jesus Christ and Paul are also included in this erroneous context, wherein Christian spiritual truths are intertwined with error. Cosmic consciousness as such, is not recognized within Christianity. It is simply not scriptural.

It would also appear that those with religious belief systems other than Christianity do not experience a relationship with their God; by which there is Father-Son spiritual communication. In authentic Christianity, the Father, the Son and the Holy Spirit dwell within the Christian. "At that day you will know the I *am* in My Father, and you in Me, and I in you." (John 14:20).

Also, [Jesus], "If anyone loves Me, he will keep My word; and My Father will love him, and We will come to him and make our home with him." (John 14:23).

Jesus told His disciples: "I am the vine, you are the branches." He also made another very powerful statement: "Without Me, you can do nothing."

Christians are blessed with the Comforter, the Holy Spirit. He is available to them for guidance at all times. The life of the authentic Christian as he journeys to spiritual maturity; is primarily directed by obedience to the Spirit from within. He is already "awake". He hears! He obeys! He receives! He gives thanks! Life can be so stress-free, relaxing, beautiful, challenging and exciting!

There is a warning from the Scriptures directed to those persons who remain uncommitted to one shepherd. Frequently, they jump from one belief or conviction to another, usually based on various cults they encounter through books they have read.

It is written: "That we should no longer be children, tossed to and fro and carried about with every wind of doctrine, by the trickery of men, in the cunning craftiness of deceitful plotting, but, speaking the truth in love." (Ephesians 4:14-15).

Whether we realize it or not, we are all engaged in some form of "spiritual warfare". We are all involved in some way. No one is untouched. We may wear any blinders we wish! The very fact that one has not taken sides reveals that one is already committed, and unconsciously *has* taken a stand. It is up to us individually to awaken to this truth, and assess where we stand, and with whom.

"Man cannot embrace neutrality through ignorance. It is not possible to be a power unto one's self, and yet claim to worship God." (From the Lost Notebooks of Wiser-Mouse).

There are many dedicated "on their own" believers. They have right-brained intuitive-thinking abilities, but one wonders which spirit imparts messages and guidance to them? Are they in bondage [slavery] to evil beliefs? And when they pray, to whom do they pray? Which God?

We are reminded by Jesus in Matthew 24:24, "For false Christs and false prophets will rise and show great signs and wonders to deceive, if possible, even the very elect. See, I have told you beforehand."

Jesus said in John 14:3: "And if I go to prepare a place for you, I will come again, and receive you unto Myself; that where I am, *there* you may be also. And where I go you know, and the way you know." Authentic Christians prepare for a recognized world to come.

Certain higher levels of consciousness where the unutterable is attained are all a part of spiritual growth. Derek Kurtis explains it beautifully in his book, *Little Boy Wild.*

"Wild Boy exclaimed, *I am* the killer whales, *I am* the dolphins! And *I am* the river, and *I am* the grizzlies". Later as he gazes into the cosmos, he asks of the star-ridden night sky: "Is it just possible that all that *is,* dwells within me already? God has placed eternity in the heart of man. Is it that these ecstatic flashes of 'I am', and 'oneness' feelings, are really experiences of being touched by God from eternity"?

In his younger days, when Wild Boy entered these states of consciousness, he explained them as his, "Theory of Simultaneous Parallel Continuity". No doubt only he knew that to which he was referring!

In another place in his book, he ecstatically exclaims: "*I am* the moon at night, *I am* Venus and the rising sun, and *I am* the coyotes too! There is just the cosmos and me; just the sun, or the stars, and the moon, and me. But *I am* the stars! *I am* the sandpipers! And *I am* the wind."

He clapped his hands and sprang to his feet.

"*I am* all things, all people, and all the animals. It's just like Walt Whitman said in his 'Leaves of Grass'. I see it now, but I could never express it to another person, because it is just as Whitman says: 'When I undertake to tell the best, I find I cannot, my tongue is ineffective on its pivots. My breath will not be obedient to its organs, I become as a dumb man'."

Paul Tillich in his *The Eternal Now* comments: "In these moments of solitude something is done to us. The centre of our being, the innermost self that is the ground of our aloneness, is elevated to the divine centre and taken into it. Therein we can rest without losing ourselves."

Gilean Douglas, in her beautiful *Silence is my Homeland,* created an enchanting record of pure wilderness life. As a naturalist she absolutely knew her flora and fauna.

She too, was taken by states of ecstatic and joyful being. Her revelations of "I am", [for me], leapt off her pages, especially as the focus of her book in no way relates to what we are exploring here.

Douglas says: "I am not the same person who waded across the Teal that first August morning. I am the deep forest; the singing rivers, the tall mountains. I am all of these things and more; I am the whole human being they have made me."

In more depth of feeling Douglas explains: "I feel that delirious sense of delight, which always comes at such moments, welling up inside me. It simply 'is' and 'I am', and that is enough. There is prayer in it and thanksgiving; there is joy, humility, a touch of sadness and the very core of peace.

I am alive in this world and the next and in all the world of space. Tree, flower and bird are my blood brothers and the golden clock of time has stopped, so that I may listen to the swift beating of my many lives.

Now I know why there is prayer: that there may be thanks given for all of this to the one Spirit who never fails to understand." Gilean Douglas is not of Time-man. She often touches the *Now* dimension.

Another confirming quote from Derek Kurtis: "Little Boy Wild still retained his 'other worldly' state of mind, I sensed his excitement and saw the star-dreams in his eyes. A family of red-headed mergansers came into view, bobbing in the swift river current; and this one little scene instantly captured and unified his current vision of 'all that is', is within me, 'I am'. He smiled".

We observe that all of the "I am" statements expressed with such passion could only be uttered by those who experience a form of unity with the Presence of God.

They originate from those persons whose spirituality is of an advanced state. Quite clearly these utterances are spiritual, but in no way do they present themselves as equality with God.

Let us examine some of the "I am" statements of our Lord Jesus Christ during His earthly tenure. They are purely spiritual:

"I am the bread of life."

"I am the light of the world."

"I am the door of the sheep."

"I am the good shepherd."

"I am the resurrection and life."

"I am the way, the truth, and the life."

"I am the true vine."

Saint Augustine said: "All words are inadequate for the expression of divine mysteries." He also made the following captivating statement: "Our use of words in which meaning is conveyed by one sound after another and never in a simultaneous present [now]; is another symptom of fallen humanity."

We probably had this ability in Eden, before the serpent did his beguiling act with the two caretakers.

Here is another Augustine gem: "My mind withdrew its thoughts from experience, extracting itself from the throng of sensuous images that it might find out what that light was wherein it was bathed … And thus, with the flash of one hurried glance, it attained to the vision of That Which Is."

In a single flash of all-encompassing comprehension; he fleetingly touched the presence of God, and became part of the "I am" oneness of that which is. He apprehended higher-space. In this "oneness" experience, he approached the omnipresence of God.

These are the unutterable flashing moments of ecstasy which are experienced within eternity. One knows beyond all doubt that death is not, and that life is eternal. No words, can ever remotely explain that contact with God in eternity.

To achieve this state of spirit, he is saying he emptied his mind of all earthly matters, including his ego, and sense of self. His spirit was seeking its home base, and sensed the light of eternity, outside of Time, and vertical to it.

In the world to come, of which Christ spoke several times, I believe we will also communicate with others in single flashes of now-vision.

The angels who spoke with man while on earth, apparently used lungs, air and vocal cords which are required in the Time-man dimension. Angels also appear to be able to eat or not eat, as they please. On their "own turf" they probably revert to now-vision and exercise angelic attributes.

Note this state of "apprehending of space" is not a feeling. It is an elevated state of being. It is quite different from anything that Time-man could possibly imagine or describe.

It is written in Acts 8:34-38, that Philip was directed by the Spirit to meet up with an Ethiopian eunuch, and preach to him about Jesus; whereupon this man of great authority was led to the water, and was baptized by Philip.

"Now when they came up out of the water, the Spirit of the Lord caught Philip away, so that the eunuch saw him no more, and he went on his way rejoicing." (Acts 8:39).

Here, Philip was "zapped" from one place to another by the Holy Spirit, within the time-dimension, probably much to the surprise and amazement of the Ethiopian *and* Philip!

There is no doubt that all the study and thinking one does about the quest for *Now,* will have a cumulative effect on comprehension. The *Now-Quest* is an obsession. It is ever in one's awareness. Whenever one is in the woods; or treading the flower-laden meadows, or, kayaking solo on a remote lake or river, one spiritually dwells within parallel worlds.

Travelling horizontally in Time is a life-long affair. Awareness, in this state of parallel being; is perceived as movement within the simultaneity of that which *"is".*

One is conscious of oneness, while being separate. It should be noted that this is not a type of brain-storming. Dimensions of consciousness change as effortlessly as: "A leaf falling on a warm autumnal day to kiss the river with gossamer touch as it flows into eternity." This is the domain of "Now-Man".

The key to entering these levels of consciousness is a complete absence of mental effort. There can be no thought processes at work, other than the Now-Quest question, which lives within the unconscious mind. In this state of receptivity, the mind is freed of all distractions.

The primary key here is to insulate, or separate one's self from the realm of Time-man. So let us now remove ourselves from the worlds of both men and time. Here is an actual complete scenario, of living the experience of being in another realm of consciousness. It is simply what happened.

It is a hot summer day in northern British Columbia. I have nothing to do, or to catch up with, in my management consulting practise for at least a week. I've discovered a remote lake. It is absolutely wild, pristine and incredibly beautiful.

This is the day that the Lord has created! There are no signs or sounds of man, because the nearest human is about forty miles away. No ranches, no farms, just natural wilderness where I can live with the animals in the forest.

I'm alone. Time-man is not here because he is alien to this dimension of consciousness. Any remaining contagion from Time-man's world always disappears when spirit, soul and body enter the isolation of wilderness. It is a state beyond the physical realm. Isolation enables effortless ascension to higher levels.

Here is the mind of pure receptivity. It welcomes the day in joyful anticipation of becoming as *one* with the cosmic and the earthly. It is a state of embracing two worlds, and being at home in both of them. One has abdicated the "I" of ego. It is not present. It has no reason to be present. In another dimension that I term *"Now"*; I am experiencing "oneness" with God and His whole creation.

"When spiritual Man has no conscious intent, the universe becomes a state of ecstatic cosmic unity. In this 'I AM' state of being, he experiences the Presence of God." (From The Lost Notebooks Wiser-Mouse).

I had been gazing out across the lake for most of the morning. Trees, lush vegetation and patches of grassy clover ran down to the water's edge. The hot summer air is alive with bird song. It is accompanied by the hum of bees among a myriad of insect sounds. I stretch fully out in a clover patch, luxuriating in absolute relaxation. Truly, this is a mystical feeling in itself. I sit up and again take up my vigil of gazing out across the lake. It is stunningly beautiful.

I had discovered upon numerous occasions, that when I relaxed thusly with no thought in mind, states of consciousness would drift one into another without my being aware of this having occurred. These transitions of consciousness are similar to the changing of scenes in a movie, where they phase in and out almost imperceptibly. One then continues in the new scene.

On this occasion, I became suddenly aware of a very tall male "being" walking on the calm water of the lake. Other beings were walking on the water also. I did not for one moment associate this figure with Jesus, or other holy beings. At that time, for me, Christianity and Bible knowledge was only in its very early stages.

I was able to watch this "being" walk in my direction for almost a minute. Then, my logical mind kicked in, disconnected me, and I was switched back into my own dimension.

I have the feeling or knowledge that I am an intruder in this scenario. If I am seen, I'm certainly not acknowledged. The beings seem to be preoccupied. How did "I" get here? Note that in these circumstances "I" am absent from my body. When the mind which runs the body, sort of on auto-pilot, observed the unreality of the situation like walking on water, "I" was reunited with my body.

This unwitting entry into another dimension is something one never forgets. There is no special interpretation. It's what happened. For me, it confirmed that there are a myriad of wave-lengths in consciousness that are unknown and unexplored. Somehow, I had tuned into one. Note that William James stated that: "Our normal waking, rational state of mind is but one type of consciousness. While all about it, parted by the flimsiest of screens, there are special levels of consciousness that are entirely different."

Experiences of this nature can be dangerous. They empower ego and increase self-reliance leading one to being a power unto one's self. Were one to yield to this temptation, one would be relegating God to second place. If a Christian should accidentally tread such strange trails, it calls for extreme caution, and due spiritual diligence.

Some years later, on another idyllic wilderness expedition with no remote thought of venturing into other levels of consciousness, another weird thing happened.

The sun was hot, and from this secluded oasis of small island tranquility, I gazed across the ocean to the far-off snow-capped mountain peaks. A light, sea-scented off-shore breeze gave welcome relief from what could have been be a scorching day.

My purpose in being here is to invest in time, to be, and to become one with the wilderness and the universe. Ruby-throated hummingbirds vie for surrounding territorial rights, including what one could describe as high-speed near-misses as they buzzed across the clearing where I lay among the fern fronds. Even the deer and horse flies seem to be absent; only the occasional hornet investigated me. It is a state beyond being just peaceful. Consciousness is in a totally neutral state. Perhaps I am not here, but this is not a recognized thought.

About an hour or so later, I found myself checking the time, and observed that the second-hand on my watch was not moving. I seemed far away as I gazed at it. Almost a minute had passed before "now reality" came to me. Again I swatted my watch, as strangely, the second-hand was still not moving.

Then, of a sudden, the second-hand sprang ahead and all was normal. A Rolex is a finely-crafted mechanical instrument that definitely does not stop and start in an erratic manner.

These watch-stopping experiences occurred many times over several years. Anyone I asked about the phenomenon looked at me with an expression that said: "You're just plain weird!" They usually made moves to extricate themselves from my immediate vicinity!

Then about eight years after the first stopped-watch experience, I had occasion to drop into a bookstore in Hawaii where I was vacationing.

There, I discovered a book that revealed the truth of the whole matter. *Itzhak Bentov* had written a delightful volume entitled, *Stalking the Wild Pendulum*, sub-titled, *On the mechanics of consciousness.* A great discovery was the chapter entitled, *An Experiment with Time.* Upon reading this, I found that my time-related experiences were real, and that neither I, nor my Rolex, were weird, or unbalanced!

Itzhak Bentov explains: "When a person has been trained by bio-feedback to produce Theta-Waves, or can put himself into a deep meditative state, and at the same time is able to watch the second hand of a clock in front of him; he will be surprised to find that the second hand has come to a stop.

It's rather a startling experience, and the natural reaction to it is, "this is impossible!" At that moment, the second hand will accelerate and resume its normal state. However, if we can get over this reaction and with half-open eyes watch the face of the clock, while all the time being in a deep meditative state, then we can keep the hand from moving for as long as we wish."

Bentov further explains: "From the moment the watch stopped to the moment it started moving again, the 'observer' was out of the body. He has the ability to flit to distant places in a fraction of a second."

So when the watch stops, [assuming that I am the observer], I've left my body to go somewhere, but where did I go? Why do I not remember where I was, in whatever dimension I had entered?

We need to be aware that it is possible, were one to continue further explorations of other dimensions of consciousness, to get caught up in acts of divination. This is an art or practice that seeks to foresee future events or discover hidden knowledge. We need to be guided by the Holy Spirit.

"In spiritual solitude Man learns that prayer shapes Eternity. Prayer is the transition of molecular-man to the ethereal in-dwelling spirit of God's love." (From the Lost Notebooks of Wiser-Mouse).

While Bentov's book was still fresh in my mind, a most humorous situation occurred. I was in my cardiologist's office where a senior cardiologist and an intern were examining me. In order to relax me while they measured blood pressure, the senior doctor asked what my current project was.

I explained to him that: "The most urgent problem I have to solve right now; is to find out where I am, when I'm not here!" The report that went to my personal physician mainly recommended that I be scheduled for a session with a psychiatrist immediately!

"What's that Steve?"

"Like ... them docs ... thinks you was real crazy like ... kinda like you was off your rocker ... an' then like ... you found you was ... not really a nut case at all ..."

"I do believe Steven, that you have the picture in a nutshell!"

There is more to man than is generally apparent. To quote Saint Augustine: "Men go abroad to wonder at the height of mountains, at the huge waves of the sea, at the long courses of the rivers, at the vast compass of the oceans, at the circular motions of the stars, and they pass themselves by without wondering."

We need to read and study our Bibles! New Christians should begin with the New Testament. A good place to start would be the Gospel of John. It is very readable, and one will discover that the future has wonders in store for us!

"But as it is written: Eye has not seen, nor ear heard, Nor have entered into the heart of man, The things which God has prepared for *them* that love him. But God has revealed *them* to us through His Spirit." (1 Corinthians 2:9-10).

Note also verse 14: "But the natural man does not receive the things of the Spirit of God, for they are foolishness to him; nor can he know *them,* because they are spiritually discerned. 15: But he that is spiritual judges all things, yet he himself is rightly judged of no man."

So just where do we go after this so-called death? Jesus said: "In My Father's house are many mansions; if it *were* not *so*, I would have told you. I go to prepare a place for you. And if I go to prepare a place for you, I will come again and receive you to Myself; that where I am, *there* you may be also." (John 14:2-4).

I have discussed mansions, and other sheep, with pastors and Christian leaders over the years. They believe that these words allude to other church organizations here on earth. All other interpretations are regarded as pure speculation.

It is written in John 10:16: "And other sheep I have, which are not of this fold; them also I must bring, and they shall hear My voice; and there will be one fold, *and* one shepherd." "And they will gather together His elect from the four winds, from one end of heaven to the other." (Matthew 24:31). (Jesus was not referring to other earthly church groups).

How limited in comprehension of God can we humans be? Have we not read in our Bibles that: "I am from above, you are from below"? "I came down" or, "My kingdom is not of this world"?

Have we not looked into the cosmos at night, to see the other worlds and mansions that our Father of lights created? Why do we place such limitations on ourselves, and especially our concept of God?

It is so appropriate that the Lord Jesus Christ refers to us as sheep. We read that: "I am the good shepherd. The good shepherd gives His life for the sheep. I am the good shepherd; and know My sheep, and am known by My own. But you do not believe, because you are not of My sheep. My sheep hear my voice, and I know them, and they follow Me." (John 10:11-27).

Here now is the crowning glory! John 10:28: "And I give them eternal life, and they shall never perish; neither shall anyone snatch them from My hand. My Father, who has given them to Me, is greater than all; and no man is able to snatch *them* out of My Father's hand. 30: I and my Father are one."

"Behold, I send you out as sheep in the midst of wolves. Therefore be wise as serpents and harmless as doves." (Matthew 10:16).

It was St. Augustine who said: "Take every opportunity to preach the Gospel, and when necessary, use words."

Each one of the millions of sheep on earth will follow the voice of his particular shepherd. So be it. Beware the myriad of belief systems, each with a different shepherd! We will follow *our* Shepherd, the Lord Jesus Christ!

CHAPTER SIX

We need to establish a common reference for the different levels of awareness and states of being, to which we have referred. In order to do so, we will temporarily place normally accepted interpretations to one side.

We have identified Time-man, as any one of we ordinary *natural-man* human beings. We live, and are locked into a chronological sequence of time from birth to death. We simultaneously live in three dimensions of space, commonly recognized as length, height and breadth. This is our everyday scenario of "time" and "space". Let us call this "Level One".

Time-man is quite conscious of time as Past, Present and Future. Level One finds Time-man following his habit of normal living, which is always hoping that his expectations for tomorrow will come to fruition. This is the function of Hope.

Time-man's future is received into his present and immediately becomes his past. He may feel no need for change. A certain seed of consciousness has yet to germinate within him. His past may contain a lot of wonderful positives. There is also a high probability that he may still suffer from unresolved problems. It is irrelevant as to what their particular labels are. He does not realize that nothing can change unless he changes it.

The fact is that he may feel powerless to prevent himself from re-winding and re-playing negative scenarios from his past. Recollections may be randomly triggered and oft-repeated. He is aware that there is more to life, but he cannot risk switching to the unknown from the more familiar and painful present.

Time-man is usually not consciously aware of the sowing and reaping principle. He has become an unwitting dweller in Level One. He has yet to be conscious of his current state of being.

Time-man in Level One, operating primarily from left-brained logic, is in a state of being that is incomplete. He has fleeting visions of change, but "glazes over" at the prospect of attempting such a task.

He comforts himself with food, sex, or other elements within his comfort zone. More likely he will just carry on in the hope that tomorrow will somehow be different from today. It will not.

We now come to Time-man's "Level Two". This level contains all of Level One, but now includes whole-brain-reality. This is where Time-man may have disciplined himself to be open and receptive to the latent inputs from his formerly somewhat dormant right-brain mind. He is discovering life-altering intuitive inputs that affect his everyday activities. Some of these communications, if he is Christian, will originate with the Holy Spirit.

Those who attain Level Two are assured of spiritual communication. Perseverance is necessary for newly-acquired habits to take effect. They may take ninety days or more to solidify.

"Level Three" is a difficult developmental phase requiring a lot of self-discipline. As Time-man goes about his everyday life, he sets himself the task of staying in his present.

He may feel victimized with the pressures of past gross errors regardless of how they originated. Frequently, he experiences them in a form of mental torture to which he has become accustomed.

He needs to deny access to these recriminations. We are suggesting that any negative intrusion of his past into his present be stopped dead in its tracks. It is imperative that he re-enter his present.

Level Three also involves conscious tongue-control. We are referring to the spoken-word. This demands constant monitoring and instant corrections.

Foundational training in Level Three is a critical step toward Level Four. Time-man is finally learning conscious control of his mental faculties, and of personal negativity. When Level Three is operating effectively, a chasm lies between his past and his present. Power will increase. Stress will decrease. Valuable psychic energy will not be expended uselessly.

"Level Four" is totally different from Levels One, Two and Three. It is as different as squirrels are from fish! Level Four cannot be recognized by Time-man without further spiritual growth. It is not of his world. Level Four is where Time-man is *not*. It is a state of being where Time does not exist.

In this state, if it *is* Time-man who has graduated, he has metamorphosed into the duality of *Now-Man*. His state of being parallels that of being "still in time", while he dwells simultaneously in the Now-dimension which is beyond time.

This dimension has no boundaries. He is now a creature who for the first time begins to recognize the true nature of the cosmic scene in which he is immersed. He is capable of consciously receiving and acting upon messages in the Now-dimension.

Now that Time-man has become *Now-Man*, the specific form of "present" he previously associated with "time", will not exist or occur for him again. His former "present" has irrevocably become that which we term "Now".

Now-Man, being vertical to, and outside of Time, has now attained the spiritual power to pivot "belief", into completed acts of *"Now-Faith"*, as a co-creator. He has reached a higher form of consciousness. This state of being is linguistically impossible to convey.

"To experience is to know. To draw aside the countless veils of consciousness one by one, yields that fragrance which empowers Man to wander among the flowers of Eternity. To see their petals open to the light of 'I AM' is His spiritual gift." *(From The Lost Notebooks of Wiser-Mouse).*

We discover in our exploration of Level Four, the person of "Little Boy Wild" explaining his ecstatic flashes of *I am*, and his experiences with theta wave scenarios. He has attained Level Four, and its stages of ecstasy, and is aware that such "states of being" carry extraordinary power. They are also linked to high accountability to our heavenly Father through our Lord Jesus Christ.

A Level Four person will daily face millions of probabilities, but not without direction. He would not have attained this state were he not absolutely responsible for his actions. If he were not ready for revelation he would not receive it.

Level Four is also where we are gifted the keys to the Kingdom. On death, [so-called], he will stay at Level Four and beyond, in as yet unidentified dimensions. This state is beyond conjecture. We can be guided only by the Holy Scriptures.

St. Augustine gives additional thought in our treatise to present, past and future, as well as eternity. He speaks of people who: "Attempt to taste eternity when their heart is still flitting about in the realm where things change, and have a past and a future and this is vain." (He is commenting on those who mix Level One Time-man with Level Four *Now-Man*).

He says: "Who can lay hold on the heart and give it fixity, so that for a little moment it may be stable, and for a fraction of time may grasp the splendour of a constant eternity." (He is referring to the flashes of "I am" that Level Four *Now-Man* experiences).

He continues: "Then it may compare eternity with temporal successiveness which never has constancy, and will see there is no comparison possible."

"In the eternal nothing is transient, but the whole is present."

"Who will lay hold on the human heart to make it still, so that it can see how eternity, in which there is neither future nor past, stands still and dictates future and past times?"

In addressing God, St. Augustine says: "You are the originator and creator of all ages. What times existed which were not brought into being by You? Or how could they pass if they never had existence?

Since, therefore, you are the cause of all times, if any time existed before you made heaven and Earth, how can anyone say you abstained from working? You have made time itself. Time could not elapse before you made time. But if time did not exist before heaven and Earth, why do people ask what you were then doing? There was no then, when there was no time.

Your years neither go nor come. Ours come and go so that all may come in succession. All your years subsist in simultaneity, because they do not change; those going away are not thrust out by those coming in. But the years that are ours will not all be until all years have ceased to be.

Your 'years' are one day, and your 'day' is not any day but today, because your 'day' does not yield to a tomorrow, nor did it fall on yesterday. Your today is eternity." (This confirms *Now-Man's* experiences of operating in Now, which is God's eternal day).

"So you begat one coeternal with you, to whom you said: 'Today have I begotten you'. You created all times and you exist before all times. Nor was there any time when time did not exist. No times are coeternal inasmuch that you are permanent. If they were permanent they would not be times. St. Augustine concludes: "What then is time? Provided that no one asks me I know, but if they do, I do not." *How about that!*

A final word from Augustine: "Take the two tenses, past and future. How can they 'be' when the past is not now present and the future is not now present? Yet if the present were always present, it would not pass into the past: it would not be time but eternity.

If then, in order to be time at all, the present is so made that it passes into the past, how can we say that present also is? So indeed we cannot truly say that time exists except in the sense that it tends toward non-existence."

Are our heads reeling yet?

Steven chortled: "Like ... like ... we ran out of time itself like ... anyways I don't have to buy no more Heinekens like ... I can just get dizzy on Augustine's stuff ..."

Let us gain some perspective. We read in Isaiah 55:8: "For my thoughts *are* not your thoughts, Nor are your ways My ways, said the Lord. 9: For *as* the heavens are higher than the earth, so are My ways higher than your ways, and My thoughts than your thoughts."

Time-man, in leaving Level Three and entering the Level Four of *Now-Man*, will need to get accustomed to shifting states of consciousness. His experience now is that his *present* alternates with his *now*, but both are contained in *Now*.

Time-man previously only had present. In Level Four it is a new type of present. It is linked to his new "Now" eternal dimension. It is not isolated. This insight allows him to recognize the pivotal-shifts within prayer that brings things into being.

Now-Man is experiencing the "gap" that lies between each thought. He understands the gap, whereas Time-man could never conceive of the probabilities within *Now-Man's* Level Four.

William James, a Harvard philosopher, named our river of thoughts and emotions as a *stream of consciousness*. Deepak Chopra states that this stream of consciousness is not made up solely of objects floating downstream; because in between every thought is a fleeting gap of silence.

Derek Kurtis in his *Little Boy Wild,* experiences a similar *gap* between thoughts. He and his friend Tim were sleeping in an old log cabin in the English woods. "Wild Boy was awakened by a beautiful bird song close by. Tim murmured,

'Nightingale', and fell asleep again. Wild Boy fell asleep also, mounting the wings of dream to blend that haunting melody with honeysuckle scent. The softer colours of those notes radiated paths to the other side of consciousness.

How many people he wondered could mount the notes of a nightingale's song and travel in search of themselves? And what might happen if a single note of that song were missing and he fell into the missing space ..."

Gaps and missing notes have intriguing similarities.

The gap, says Chopra: "... turns out to be a central player if one is interested in what lies beyond normal thought. Every fraction of a second we are permitted a glimpse into another world, one that is inside us and yet obscurely out of reach. Infinite gaps full of intelligence, dimensions and parallel worlds are within us."

It is we who direct our life by the choices we make. We can only apprehend the gap, or *Now,* when we are at Level Four. If we have difficulty in comprehending those things above us, and within us, know that *He* is from *above* and we are from *below*. We are reminded that we are always subject to the spiritual levels above us.

"Man needs to be aware of his sanctified spiritual routes to the kingdoms of God. Only men of Godly intent and the purest spirit of 'I AM', may enter the portals of Eternity." (From the Lost Notebooks of Wiser-Mouse).

It may be inconsequential to any Christian, as to which of the levels we have explored actually applies to him. We are all at different levels of comprehension throughout our entire journey on Earth. However, these levels may act as guides or markers to reflect spiritual states of progress. The

Christian odyssey is never static, on hold, or repetitive over long periods of time.

The relevant common denominator which links we Christians, is our personal relationship with our heavenly Father, our Lord Jesus Christ, and the Holy Spirit. We return to the fact that this commonality is *"prayer"*. Our text explores further elements of prayer through the eyes of an authentic Christian.

It is essential to reiterate the basics of prayer. The central focus of the authentic Christian's spiritual life is that of communicating with God. The most important lesson we can learn is, *how to pray.*

We are not taught this in our Christian assemblies. It is usually assumed by the pastor that the congregation knows how to pray. He says: "Let us pray", and the service proceeds. We endeavour to wear holy expressions and close our eyes.

In the churches that practice institutionalized religion, most of the "prayer-stuff" is taken care of for us. Often, this operates with fixed responses to the holy utterances of the preacher. Eventually, we are saved by the command that we may now sit, which we do with a quiet sigh of relief.

So where do we go from here? We need to reinforce our understanding of prayer. We have seen that this matter of praying is not to be taken lightly. It is foundational to Christianity.

So we come perhaps to the primary prayer question which is why do we *not* pray? What is it that hinders us? Is it simply that we do not know how to pray or how to achieve a God-connection"?

Our first step is to believe that God *IS!* This is not an intellectual matter. It is a spiritual matter. We are about to pray, and in so doing we withdraw from our ego-selves. Our mindset is not centred on self or others.

We come to God in a state of selfless humility, an act of total emptying and surrender to a higher power. It is an act of openness, trust, innocence and receptivity. Yes, it is child-like, and this state of being establishes communication with God.

God is Spirit, so we pray in the Spirit. What does that mean? We offer to this maybe as yet unknown God, the true intent of our hearts. We need to know God personally, and to experience His grace, love, and forgiveness, which yield the peace which surpasses all understanding. Power and beauty dwell in our surrender to God. We listen and obey. We always need to pray with a child-like spirit. This is a simplistic state, devoid of, and unencumbered by the warped conceptions of adulthood.

The second step is for us to determine as to whom we pray. Christians are shocked to learn that the Bible does *NOT* teach us to pray our petitions directly to Jesus, nor to the Holy Spirit. Also, the oft repeated term "Lord" can increase confusion—inasmuch that it can mean either the Father or the Son. Most Christian leaders follow a "blended" prayer approach, wherein they alternately pray to all three individuals of the Trinity.

Many regard this as heresy. [Heresy is any teaching that is contrary to the Bible]. Most churches attempt to validate their 'changing of the Scriptures', by lengthy, convoluted explanations. The choice however, is ours! Do we obey the Word of God? Or do we follow the heretic traditions of Man?

Authentic Christians are obedient to the teaching of Christ in the Bible. They address their requests *ONLY* to the Father— in the Name of Jesus.

In John.14:14—Jesus said, "If you will ask anything in My name, I will do it." His teaching is equally definitive in John.15:7, 15:16, 16:23, 16.24, and 16.26. Jesus' statements are immutable. It is written in John.13:35. "The Scriptures cannot be broken."

Our failure to obey Jesus' prayer instructions can be attributed to the almost total lack of understanding among Christians and their leaders as to what the phrase, 'IN MY NAME' actually means. Frequently, pastors pray directly to Jesus, and then close those same prayers with, "We ask this in Jesus' name." This begs the question—to whom were they praying then? *It is not possible to pray to directly to Jesus—in His name—when one is personally addressing Jesus.* Basic English and Elementary Christianity rule this out! Our Lord Jesus Christ fully explains the meaning of '*IN MY NAME*', in Amp. John.14.26.

When we pray *TO* the *FATHER*, we do not do so of our own cognizance—but under the jurisdiction and authority of *JESUS*. We appear before the Father in Jesus' Name and power. The Father reacts to us, not on the basis of who one is, but as the person who sent you, [Jesus]. It is Jesus addressing the Father through us. [No, we are not Jesus].

Under such representation we are possessed of Jesus' authority. We are acting on Jesus' behalf. We act in His stead. It's similar to acting under a Power of Attorney. This is the meaning of '*IN MY NAME*'.

Okay—so what's a Power of Attorney? In the world of Law— it's a legal written document. In this case we're referring to the Bible—in which one person—Jesus, appoints another person, a Believer, Disciple or Apostle; to act on His behalf. Authority is conferred on that person, and by that authority he also receives power to perform certain acts or functions on behalf of the Principal—Jesus.

Legally speaking, a Power of Attorney expires at the death of the one who created it. [But this only applies to Man]. In our context—Jesus is alive and sitting at the right hand of the Father.

Jesus explains His meaning of "in My name" in Amp. John.14:26, when he speaks of the Holy Spirit. Note the, "in My place", to represent Me", and to, "act on My behalf— they all mean "in My name". They have nothing to do with praying directly to Jesus. Jesus did NOT teach us to "Ask of Me."

The Bible even instructs us to *THANK* our heavenly Father in Jesus' name. Ephesians 5:20: "At all times and for everything giving thanks *IN THE NAME* of our Lord Jesus Christ *TO* God the Father."

Further, the scriptures do not instruct us, or teach us to worship, or pray to any man of an ecclesiastical standing. Nor are we taught by Jesus to pray to, or through, the saints, the Virgin Mary, or the Holy Spirit. Jesus instructed us to pray to the Father, in His name.

Jesus gives us a format, an example of how to pray in Matthew 6:9: "In this manner, therefore, pray: Our Father in heaven, Hallowed be Your name. 10: Your kingdom come. Your will be done On earth as *it is* in heaven. 11: Give us this day our daily bread.

12: And forgive us our debts, as we forgive our debtors. 13: And do not lead us into temptation, But deliver us from the evil one. For Yours is the kingdom, and the power and the glory forever. Amen."

Jesus continues, 14: "For if you forgive men their trespasses, your heavenly Father will also forgive you. 15: But if you do not forgive men their trespasses, neither will your Father forgive your trespasses."

Jesus simply says, pray along these lines; use them as a guide. The Lord's Prayer is powerful and all-inclusive.

We need to observe that: "Whoever denies the Son does not have the Father either; he who acknowledges the Son has the Father also." (1 John 2:23). Then in 1 John 5:12: "He who has the Son has life, he who does not have the Son of God does not have life."

These Scriptures give us a clear picture of the Spirit of Truth, and are revelatory of exposing religious cults which do not recognize Jesus as Lord. These cults pray to God directly, and bypass acknowledgement of the Son. This is a true mixing of truth with error.

In John 3:35, we are given a clear view of the Father's delegated authority to His Son, including judgement day. "The Father loves the Son, and has given all things into His hand." So now we know exactly where we stand!

Many Christians have fallen into a self-effacing, "I'm unworthy" mode of thinking, with both church, and God. After coming to Christ, they still sing hymns about being downcast wretches! Is it just false humility? Where is the joy and happiness of being a new creature in Christ?

In sharp contrast, authentic Christians "stand tall", in humility and spiritual power. They are the Spiritual sons of God. There is nothing unworthy or wretched about a true son of God.

Authentic Christians hold their heads high, not in false pride, but as ambassadors for the kingdom of God, in filled by the Holy Spirit. When man speaks through the Holy Spirit, it is with the same authority as God. The pivotal-shift in the Spirit of man ensures his abdication of self. It is not man addressing a situation, it is God.

We now need to explore a common prayer phrase known to all of us; it is: "If it be Thy will". Authentic Christians are committed to pray in the power of faith. They are *not* subject to elements of doubt or disbelief in the prayer process. Such would be the case if they used the term, "if it be Thy will", for the very nature of that phrase tends to leave us open for doubts, wavering, and the negation of faith.

But hold on there! When we examine that phrase: "If it be thy will Lord", we run into two schools of doctrine, [teaching], on this matter, that appear to be diametrically opposed! It is claimed that, "If it be Thy will", is an expression of humility, or "Your will be done Lord", as in the Lord's Prayer. This could give the impression that our petitions are really self-cancelling, that God is going to do what He wants to do anyway. This leaves us in the pathetic and impotent situation of begging for what may never be brought to fruition.

Spiritual sons of God are not required to beg. God will hear and not ignore the petitions of His Spiritual sons. Nor will he necessarily grant them! God will, however, give us direction through the Holy Spirit. Biblical evidence is that wonders and "miracles" are achieved through praying correctly.

So let us examine the prayers of *natural-soul-man*, [who may not be "in-the-Spirit"]. He may not take Jesus at His Word. He introduces doubts and 'wavering', by tagging his petitions with, "If it bc Thy will", along with repetitive, "We just ask", phrases of apparent humility, but without any real expectations of receiving.

The prayers of authentic Christians are powered by unwavering faith, based on their experience of receiving. Dwelling in the Presence of God, they honour that doctrine portrayed in 1 John 5:14-15, namely: "Now this is the confidence we have in Him, that if we ask anything according to His will, He hears us. And if we know that He hears us, whatever we ask, we know we have the petitions we asked of Him."

When authentic Christians pray, they do so according to His will. The Holy Spirit intercedes with the Father in our prayers. He then imparts the will of God to us, as it applies to our lives or any current project that we may have underway.

Christians do not dictate, or request, any time-frames in the granting of their petitions. Having prayed to the Father in Jesus' Name, they give thanks for they have received. This is *Now-Faith* in action. Prayer requests are "bringing into being, things that were not".

God is Spirit, and we need to pray in the Spirit, but how? Immature Christians and many others may never have received any effective prayer instruction. Not knowing how to pray according to the Scriptures, is negligence on the part of the assembly, and of the pastor. This results from lack of cohesiveness among the members. They are not living in unity, as part of the Body of Christ.

"Man has yet to learn how to enter the Presence of God. He needs to be indwelt by the Holy Spirit and devoid of 'self'. Only then will he be empowered to receive." (From the Lost Notebooks of Wiser-Mouse).

For the record, our doctrine of choice in relation to effective and fervent prayer in this text, is to preclude the phrase, "If it be Thy will."

Although we pray to the Father, this does not isolate us from praising Jesus. In prayer; we give praise, and thanks, for all He has done for us, including His ultimate sacrifice, that of dying on the Cross. We may speak with Him on numerous matters not related to "asking". Being of the Trinity, He is fully aware at all times of our prayer requests and communication with the Father. Jesus is our Lord, our teacher, our Intercessor and our ultimate judge on judgement day.

Our third step in approach to prayer is, where do we pray? Inasmuch that God is everywhere, [omnipotent], we are not limited to any location on Earth. We can pray anywhere, in our private places, be they in the woods, or parks, on the street, or in our vehicles, because He is within us. God does not just dwell in that church structure up the road. Churches are places wherein we learn, grow, and develop in Christian fellowship.

How strange it is that many Christians may be enshrouded in holy feelings upon entering a church, cathedral or other place of worship, but upon leaving, these same feelings depart! Surely the holy feelings should be within us, before, and after, any contact with a specific Christian congregational structure.

Our heavenly Father is with us wherever we go. There should be no on-off line of demarcation. If there is, it is a spiritual-marker of some high significance that needs to explored and changed. Did we really leave God behind in that building? Was it He in the colourful robes? Was that Him on the featured cross?

Is church really just God neatly wrapped and packaged by man to serve tradition? It is sad to bring these observations into the light of that which Jesus taught.

In Matthew 15:6, Jesus, in addressing the scribes and Pharisees, warns us against following the traditions of men. He asked: "Why do you transgress the commandment of God because of your tradition?" The religious leaders of Jesus' day were careful to keep their traditions. In so doing, they omitted the very matters God had commanded.

How rather similar this is to the operation of man-made religions operating today. The landscape is dotted with "Christian" churches, wherein they worship tradition rather than God. In so doing, they negate the eternal truth of God's Word. Large congregations give blind support to mammon in robes of unrighteousness, and the Holy Scriptures are reduced to the fables of man.

We need to learn how to actually talk with God. If we listen, we'll hear Him speak to us. We need an intimate relationship *with* Him, not just to know *about* Him. In every circumstance of life, prayer is the most natural outpouring of the soul.

"Saying a prayer" has nothing to do with communicating with God. Genuine prayer is actual contact with God. The Lord's Prayer should not come forth mechanically as in saying a "memorized" prayer. Depending on the focus of our mindset, we could well be reciting: "Mary had a little lamb".

We need to avoid automated prayers. They may have originated with the Pharisees, and others associated with vain repetitions. However, it is said that fervent and effective prayer, is the most neglected element in all of Christianity.

Prayer needs to become habitual. Many people believe in prayer, but not many pray. Few of us have ever experienced the power of prayer at work in our lives. Plant success, reap success.

Accumulated prayer achievements will give us greater faith, apart from enjoying the fruits of our requests. Our Heavenly Father desires a praying people who are willing, humble and obedient. Jesus said: "Ask and it shall be given you; seek, and you shall find; knock, and it will be opened to you." (Matthew 7:7).

"Godly contact is a flowing river of spiritual wisdom. Man may navigate these prayer-waters powered only by selfless love, faith and humility. It is here where Man the created, speaks with his Creator." (From the Lost Notebooks of Wiser-Mouse).

This whole matter of prayer is not difficult! It is so easy to pray to our heavenly Father. We do not need prayer books, beads, candles, images, symbols, lucky rabbit's feet or any other distractions. These prayer-aids enslave us to the worshipping of man-made church traditions, not God. Prayer crutches have a surreal mix of fact and phantasy devoid of spirituality. God is spirit and we worship Him in spirit.

Here is a prayer setting. In humility, on our knees, [if we can manage that], or just standing in the privacy of our prayer closet, we simply bring our normal "rotten, soiled, sordid" selves to God.

We do not have to articulate our sins, He knows of them already. "Though your sins be as scarlet, They shall be white as snow." (Isaiah 1:18).

Jesus looks at the intent in our hearts. He loves us unconditionally, no matter what we have become. So let us pray often, and praise our Heavenly Father. Whether we are aware of it or not, asking, is the rule of the kingdom. Most of us quit praying at the point where we ought to begin.

Prayer is usually born out of a desperate need, a response to an impossible situation. It is quite rarely an involuntary prayer of praise. The more often we pray in humility and faith, the more often we'll see our prayers granted. God's promise is: "Call to Me, and I will answer you, and show you great and mighty things, which you do not know." (Jeremiah 33:3).

Effective prayer requests are simply our asking of God in the Name of Jesus, in humility, love, innocence and expectancy, like little children. That is how simple it can be!

"The prayers of authentic Christians rise spontaneously before God. They encompass only the pure intent of their hearts." (From the Lost Notebooks of Wiser-Mouse).

Christians consistently offer faithless, misdirected petitions to our heavenly Father, including requests for the forgiveness of sins. Many of these prayers are ineffective, due to our lack of instruction on how to pray in the manner that Jesus outlined in the Scriptures. However, Jesus will never overlook the cry and intent of the human heart truly seeking forgiveness. It is not lost. Jesus is cognizant of our every condition, motive and reason for praying.

We may seek relief from the weight of sin and wrong-doing in our lives, and eventually realize there must be a better way to journey through life. Being unaware of the power of God's forgiveness, we may continue to flounder in debt, ill-health or other problematic situations. We may even find ourselves consulting a psychiatric professional, rather than God. This critical matter may cause us to explore the power of forgiveness.

Our heavenly Father freely forgives us in the name of Jesus. So also we need to freely forgive any other person of sins committed against us [real or imagined] with no exclusions.

If we fail to relinquish all sin whether by thought, word or deed, with no reservations, we will have placed our heavenly Father in the position of denying *us* forgiveness.

"Man under the power of sin, without confession, isolates himself from God. In humility, he petitions God for forgiveness, in the name of Jesus." (From the Lost Notebooks of Wiser-Mouse).

Error, sin and guilt separate Christians from God. In the Presence of the Father, in the name of Jesus, they confess, receive forgiveness, and give thanks. One always gives thanks for that which one has received.

We need to be very much aware that if one cannot give thanks, we may have unwittingly or consciously retained sin. Inasmuch that we have not sown forgiveness, neither have we received forgiveness. What are we holding back, and why? Confession is total cleansing, not sin held back in part or in whole.

There is a pivotal-shift-point in this cleansing process, whereby we are changed from being as "scarlet", to being "white as snow", through the shed blood of Jesus on the cross.

Once this state has been attained, it negates any need or requirement to dwell in, or focus on previous sin and guilt. Were one to do so, they would be empowering, or re-empowering sin.

Either by lack of knowledge, or habit, many Christians fail to recognize this pivotal-shift-point of receiving forgiveness, and being freed of sin. As a result, while still in the Presence of the Father; they continue to focus on that which is *past* darkness, rather than the now spiritual purity of self, attained through Christ's forgiveness.

Forgiveness born of confession enables the wellspring of the human Spirit to dwell within the Presence of God. Again, the Holy Spirit gently brings Scripture to mind with: "For *there* is one God, and one Mediator between God and men, *the* Man Christ Jesus." (1 Timothy 2:5).

We need always to be aware of the danger in our being habitually submissive; and therefore willing to permit ecclesiastics and others, to act for us in religious spiritual matters. This is a form of enslavement.

No church can assume that it has been gifted the power to rob man of direct contact with God. If such were the case, these powers would originate from a source other than our heavenly Father.

God says in Jeremiah 29:13: "And you will seek Me and find *Me*, when you search for Me with all your heart." It is with this verse in mind, and this intent, that we approach prayer. Let us take a look at what James says about our reasons and manner of praying. We need to observe the results.

"Where do wars and fights *come* from among you? Do *they* not *come* from your *desires for* pleasure that war in your members? You lust and do not have. You murder and covet and cannot obtain. You fight and war. Yet you do not have because you do not ask. You ask and do not receive, because you ask amiss, that you might spend it on your pleasures. Adulterers and adulteresses! Do you not know that friendship with the world is enmity with God?" (James 4:1-4).

Let us recall the two critical rules of praying that James gave us; *not asking*, and *asking in the wrong way.* We need to pray effectively, with spiritual comprehension. If we have not prayed correctly, we have not prayed at all! James succinctly says: "The purpose of prayer is to commune with God". If we don't connect, the prayer is useless.

"For life to become a living prayer, Man's connection with God needs to be unbroken. As yet, most of Mankind has to transition from incompleteness in 'time' to wholeness in the Eternal realm." (From the Lost Notebooks of Wiser-Mouse).

Prayer has a long scriptural history of being effective. Prayer has stopped the sun in its course, even causing it to go *back* by ten degrees. (Isaiah 38:7). Prayer has cured sickness, cast out devils, increased grace, increased faith and obtained forgiveness.

We see in Hebrews 11:33-35: "Who through faith subdued kingdoms, worked righteousness, obtained promises, stopped the mouths of lions, quenched the violence of fire, escaped the edge of the sword, out of weakness were made strong, became valiant in battle, turned to flight the armies of the aliens. Women received their dead raised to life again."

James says that the effective fervent prayer of a righteous man brings great results. All things are available to man through prayer.

"Man is exhorted to pray without ceasing. He is endowed with grace and power to achieve this. His prayer-life creates a living-bridge with Eternity." (From the Lost Notebooks of Wiser-Mouse).

The Bible urges us to pray with all manner of prayer, and to use every kind of prayer and entreaty, and at every opportunity, pray in the Spirit."

It is said that a man whose prayers are few, short and feeble, must be a man in low spiritual condition. We can do nothing without prayer. In some cases, Christians may have to be aware of the power of importunate praying. What on earth is that? "Importunate", means persistent in request or demand, to the point of being troublesome.

An excellent example is in Luke 18:2: "There was in a certain city a judge who did not fear God nor regard man. 3: Now there was a widow in that city; and she came to him, saying, 'Get justice for me from my adversary'.

4: And he would not for a while; but afterward he said within himself, 'Though I do not fear God, nor regard man, 5: yet because this widow troubles me, I will avenge her, lest by her continual coming she weary me'."

Steven interjected: "Like ... He's like talkin' about ... the squeaky wheel gets the grease like?"

"You have it Steven! Persistent prayer works. What were you saying about Bambi a moment of two ago?"

"Like ... like ... I dunno how to pray like ... but I'm thankful ... when I shoot a Bambi ... an' I got food like ... I sorta ... look up in the sky and say ... thank you ... because like ... he made them Bambi too ... an' he's feedin' me."

"God loves you too Steven. He knows when you're making Bambi stew, and He is aware that you are thankful! He would like you to know Him better. Not just talking about Him, but talking with Him in prayer."

Ken Hagen says: "The Bible teaches several kinds of prayer, and different rules governing them." We Christians make the mistake in not differentiating between them. Brother Hagen lists eight types of prayers:

They are the prayer of faith, the prayer of consecration, the prayer of commitment, of worship, of agreement, of prayer in the Spirit, united prayer, and intercessory prayer. When we seriously examine all these prayer types, we may be able to grasp the full power of prayer.

"Steven! You look confused!"

"Like ... like ... you mean we got prayin' rules an' stuff like? S'pose I get mixed up like ... and prays the wrong way like?"

"Steve, there are no rules. It comes from your heart. He'll understand." Steven was concentrating on the final stages of cleaning his rifle. So I concluded with, [much to his evident relief], "So really Steven, it's relatively easy to pray effectively."

He threw another log on the fire, and after taking a deep breath, suggested we open a couple of beers to quench our thirsts after such a long dissertation. Indeed, it was with a sigh that I too perched on a mossy log to succumb to the silence of our solitude. Inasmuch that bottled liquid has a tendency to obey gravity, I gazed high into the cosmos. It was a time for quiet contemplation.

I pondered the question: "How can one effectively transmit to another, the wisdom and insight of all that one has spiritually experienced?" We are all at entirely different levels of comprehension. But this question lacked validity in the Holy plans of God. Was I not intruding on the "turf" of the Holy Spirit? How many times had I counselled: "Relax, listen, and obey His instructions!" Then, swift as a peregrine falcon in full earthward stoop, the Word came. "Go thou and do likewise!"

Alfred Lord Tennyson wrote an excellent poem worthy of our slow consideration:

"More things are wrought by prayer
Than this world dreams of.

Wherefore, let your voice
Rise like a fountain for me night and day.
For what are men better than sheep or goats,
That nourish a blind life within the brain,
If, knowing God, they lift not hands of prayer
Both for themselves and those who call them friend?
For so the whole round earth is in every way
Bound by gold chains about the feet of God."

Bible reading and prayer comprise our life-belt. We cannot just "float" on our own. That is man-made thinking [originating from the soul]. It is about relying on ourselves.

The following verses, establish the firm stand and precedent that Jesus established in relation to scriptural authentic Christianity. There is nothing *soft* in the penalty outlined for disobedience to His Word. Jesus' words have a foundation of great beauty, filled with the promise of eternal life.

It is written in John 15:1: "I am the true vine, and My Father is the vinedresser. 2: Every branch in Me that does not bear fruit He takes away; and every *branch* that bears fruit He prunes, that it may bear more fruit. 3: You are already clean because of the word which I have spoken to you.

4: Abide in Me and I in you. As the branch cannot bear fruit of itself, unless it abides in the vine, neither can you, unless you abide in Me. 6: If anyone does not abide in Me, he is cast out as a branch and is withered; and they gather them and throw them into the fire, and they are burned."

Jesus is saying, show intent, progress or results, or be burned up.

Steven frowned. "Like you was just sayin' like ... we is gonna get burned up, unless we turns over a new leaf like."

"Yes Steven. There's going be a conflagration."

179

"Like a jeazly big fire like?" "Yes!" I replied"

I like ... don't wanna be firewood like. I'd sooner ... be sittin' round the fire like ... and sippin' wine. It's a no-brainer ..."

"Yes Steve! But why is it that we have such difficulty in understanding Jesus' teachings? I believe that above all, we need to ask our heavenly Father for wisdom, and comprehension. We need to pray and obey".

E. M. Bounds on Prayer, is one of several excellent studies on the definitive subject of prayer. To quote a miniscule example, he says:

"Prayer is simply the expression of faith."

"The great business of praying is a hurried, petty, starved, beggarly business with most men."

"Prayer does not stand alone. It comes as a result of a vigorous and commanding faith."

"No man can pray, really pray, who does not obey."

"Child of God, can you pray? Are your prayers answered? If not, why not? Answered prayer is the proof of your *real* praying."

Paul's teaching, is that praying is the most important of all activities on earth. Even authentic Christians can, and do fail in their prayer mission. We all need to consistently review the basic elements of Christianity. To be immersed in the scriptures, is our pathway to the emulation of Christ.

We need also to clearly understand who and what we are in relation God. To acquire this spiritual knowledge, is to attain the state of "peace" which surpasses all earthly comprehension!

We have so much for which to be thankful. Here is a powerful scripture that fills Christians with unspeakable joy. It is the scriptural focus on our exact relationship with our Lord Jesus Christ.

It is found in John 15:16: "You did not choose Me, but I chose you and appointed you that you should go and bear fruit, and that your fruit should remain, that whatever you ask the Father in My name He may give you."

Note that we are appointed and ordained of God. We have been chosen!

CHAPTER SEVEN

During the Christian spiritual walk there will be times when we feel somewhat helpless in the face of problems that appear to be insurmountable. Christians, indeed all of us, are often in need of additional power to manage life itself. This is where we need to know the innermost workings of *grace.* It is a source of gifted spiritual power that we may draw upon, but with which most Christians are not actively familiar.

Man rarely experiences the power of Grace. Without active knowledge of what grace is, and what grace does, Man cannot even approach an understanding of God's nature.

The Scriptures declare in John 1:17: "For the law was given by Moses, but grace and truth came by Jesus Christ." To gain knowledge of grace and its supernatural power is of one of the great core truths that is exclusive to Christianity.

Over the years, upon occasion I have asked Christian leaders: "What exactly is Grace?" This question is usually met with frowns of recall, and finally: "Well, it's God's unmerited favour." Some go further, to explain that He bestows upon us all kinds of good things that we really do not deserve. We are without merit, but He gifts us anyway.

However, we will see that grace is so much more! We need to experience Grace. We have to be conscious of Grace in order to develop it. Authentic Christians see grace as God's fully expressed infinite love. Christians have failed to make grace a priority in their lives. Grace is an unrecognized spiritual gift of our heavenly Father. We are needful of its latent power. That is why it is offered.

However, it is indeed rare to experience grace in action anywhere. The entire subject of grace and its workings are too extensive to include in this brief treatise. We will only be highlighting the recognizable elements of grace.

"Grace flows from the fountain of God's love. It is Man's indwelt Godly power awaiting his recognition. It empowers him to face all problems. It is Man, in thought, word, and deed, gifting love to Man." (From the Lost Notebooks of Wiser-Mouse).

Grace is *not* that power of God which produces physical healing. Nor is it the power of God that brings a miracle or alters situations. [That would be the *Now-Faith* we have examined]. Grace *is* however, the power of God which works specifically in the inner-man. The more we are aware of God's grace, the more we are removed from the judging of other people. We are able to accept them as they are.

Grace enables us to go *through* situations, not to be delivered *from* them. Grace does not change situations, it changes *people*. *Now-Faith* is designed to move mountains; but Grace gifts us the power to go over, around, or through, situations that cannot be changed. Paul's example validates this.

We will recall that Paul complained to the Lord three times about the "thorn in his side", [a problem]. "And He said to me, My grace is sufficient for you, for My strength is made perfect in weakness. Therefore, I take pleasure in infirmities, in reproaches, in needs, in persecutions, in distresses for Christ's sake. For when I am weak, then I am strong." (2 Corinthians 12:9-18).

Grace empowers the believer for confrontation of problems. This is the gift of grace. It empowers us! God has already given every one of us, "the measure of grace". If the going gets really tough, we have the exhortation: "Let us therefore come boldly to the throne of grace, that we obtain mercy and find grace to help in time of need." (Hebrews 4:16).

Grace enables us to bear up under trouble manfully. But we also discover that no one deserves grace. It is not an entitlement. The fruits of spiritually gifted grace are inestimable.

Grace is the unconditional acceptance of our fellow man. We are mostly meeting with regular everyday sinners like ourselves; in the market place, the church or elsewhere. Grace is freely given *by* us *to* those with whom we interact. It is spiritually imparted. God gifts grace freely to us.

Philip Yancy's, *What's So Amazing About Grace?*, is an in-depth study on grace that gives us beautiful insight on the workings of grace and its power. Yancy states: "Grace is the church's great distinctive. It's the one thing the world cannot duplicate and the one thing it craves above all else, for only grace can bring hope and transformation to a jaded world."

In Richard Blackaby's, *Putting a Face on Grace*, he says: "Grace is functional to everything God does in our lives." He identifies the attributes of *Grace* in a simple and powerful manner. We cannot fail to apprehend its meaning when he says: "Grace is a gift of kindness given to someone who does not deserve it. Grace is not reciprocal, it goes one way. Grace is costly; someone has to pay for grace". (Meaning that egoism needs to be dethroned).

Other elements of grace so elegantly captured are: "Grace looks at what people can become and seeks to help them reach their potential. Grace focuses on solutions, not problems. Grace leads to action. Grace is what motivates God to relate to us moment by moment with perfect love."

"God looks at us through the eyes of grace. If He did not, we would have no hope. Grace is a lubricant that eases friction in any relationship. God expects the best but offers freedom to fail. Grace celebrates success and does not keep score of wrongs."

Do we still believe that we are on our own in this matter? It is written: "No temptation has overtaken you except such as is common to man; but God is faithful, who will not allow you to be tempted beyond what you able, but with the temptation will also make a way of escape, that you may be able to bear it." (1 Corinthians 10:13).

God knows. He is way ahead of us. He created us. This tells us that God is, within the context of any situation, aware of our individual strengths, weaknesses and breaking-points. He then creates alternatives, thereby providing choices for us. Whether our choice is correct or otherwise, whatever our decision, it is born of our free-will. Ultimately, we are responsible and accountable for our actions.

Some texts may so overstress all-encompassing grace that one comes away with the impression that "anything goes". One can do whatever one wishes throughout life; all is always forgiven under grace. [Let's go ahead and sin, we can always ask for forgiveness later]. Not so!

Paul says, in Romans 6:1: "What shall we say then? Shall we continue in sin, that grace may abound? 2: Certainly not! How shall we who died to sin live any longer in it?" There is no way we can be under the gift of grace, and act as if we had a licence to sin.

Now let us look at Matthew 21:12: "Then Jesus went into the temple of God and drove out all those who bought and sold in the temple, and overturned tables of the money changers and the seats of those who sold doves. 13: And He said to them, 'It is written, *My house shall be called a house of prayer,* but you have made it a *den of thieves'.*"

Truth and Grace came by Jesus Christ. This is a classic case of He who brought grace to us, clearly demonstrating with a scourge, [whip]; that evil shall not, and cannot be condoned under a shield of grace.

When we are faced with gross abuse of grace, we have the legal right as ambassadors for Christ to correct such matters. In doing so, we would be acting out of objective judgement, [not criticism]. This is spiritually correct.

"Throw another log on the fire Steven, and we'll try to take the mystery out of it! We have to follow a few simple rules."

"Like … you can't get away with nothin' like … you mean we can't sin like … an' hide under this grace stuff … without gettin' zapped … or somethin'?"

"Yes", I replied.

Grace must come into action *before* temptation pivots into the committing of the sin, which is yielding to the sin. At this critical juncture we see in James 4:6: "But He gives more grace. Therefore He says: God resists the proud, but gives grace to the humble."

In the Old Testament, we read about Joseph, he of the robe of many colours, and much favoured by his father Jacob. In Egypt, Joseph was in charge of a rich man's household, a man called Potiphar. It was here that he was subjected to the adulterous desire of Potiphar's wife. When Joseph was approached by her, he says in effect: "Would you have me commit this great sin, [fornication], in the presence of God?"

Note the power of grace entering prior to the potential yielding to sin. The rest is history. She ripped off his shirt and he fled from her. (Genesis 39:12).

Joseph's "Gatekeeper" would not permit, [which was for him], an open display of sin in God's presence. Grace empowered him. Joseph lived in "Level Four" awareness, and he prayed in Now-Faith. He was obedient to his Gatekeeper. This obedience is born out of trust which has become absolute.

"Trust is faith in full bloom. Trust is the most felt of all the spiritual qualities. It only works through love. Whereas hope expects, trust receives." (From the Lost Notebooks of Wiser-Mouse).

Many people are staggered by the very simplicity of trust. They look for some great thing to come to pass, while all the time: *"The word is near you, in your mouth and in your heart."* (Romans 10:8).

We now need to return to this critical matter of obedience. We learned that obedience is an element of love and of *Now-Faith* in action. We must not confuse the word "obedience" with the typical supermarket or restaurant obedience scenario.

This is when the kids are pulling stuff off the grocery shelves, or poking people in the next booth at a café, and tearing around the place. The mother finally yells in frustration at Jimmy: "I told you not to do that. You're not listening!" (This type of admonition is so ingrained in our culture that it may never change!).

He is listening, but he is not obeying. There is more to this than meets the ear. He hears perfectly well. Hearing is the *first* part. Listening is the *second* part which is receiving the message. Obeying is the *third* part. This critical linkage is missing! Listening and obeying have two distinctly different meanings. We need to be exact.

Why are we so loath to use that word "obey"? Is it that individually, we are reluctant to abdicate the throne of self? If so, we are at square one, again!

Many Christians have no concept of obedience. We need to be forewarned. Disobedience often has dire consequences, sometimes of a lethal nature. Let us not ever confuse listening with obeying. Hearing should trigger the pivotal-shift into obedience.

Authentic Christians are always listening for messages from the Holy Spirit. It takes some fine-tuning and awareness to identify these incoming messages. When they are received, it calls for our unquestioning obedience. Too often, we have learned the hard way that we need to obey immediately.

In the matter of effective and sensible communication, there is much to be learned. It's time we observed ourselves saying something out of habit incorrectly, when we mean something quite different. [Our Christian assemblies also have this problem]. When these unconscious acts of incorrect language usage are brought to our attention, we defend ourselves by saying: "Well, everyone knows what we really mean!" Not so!

Gilean Douglas, in her *Silence is my Homeland,* also comments on this vital matter of speech and understanding: "Words are meant to be ties of communication, but now they have become barriers of misunderstanding.

We have forgotten the true meaning of so many words. Even those we do use are used so indiscriminately, that the power is taken out of them to the point where they contain nothing of any value."

Douglas continues: "It would appear that we should watch our words more carefully than ever before. We must ask ourselves the real meaning of each word before we use it. If we could only realize the power and wealth and beauty of words, we would treasure them like jewels, bringing them out one by one to adorn the lovely garments of silence."

Our entire lives rely on our ability to communicate effectively. The inability to do so creates much stress and depression. We need to manage our lives, not let our lives manage us! A change is indicated, and only *we* can do this. Most authentic Christians do enjoy a stress-free life.

The famous twelve-step prayer that originated with AA is a powerful guide to keep all of us on track: "God grant me the serenity to accept the things I cannot change, [grace], the courage to change the things I can, and the wisdom to know the difference."

When did we last experience serenity? When did we last consciously relax every muscle in our bodies? Have we yet observed that a lot of the time we are so tense that we are hardly breathing? Courage! These problems are common to all of us.

Every time we worry, or agonize over something, it is a vote against God. It is an unconscious vote for satanic power. What are we concerned with or worried sick about? What is it that we fear? Why are we empowering it? To whom or to what are we yielding? Who is in control? Fear always brings Satan on the scene. Faith brings God on the scene.

Paul says: "And do not yield your members *as* instruments of unrighteousness to sin, but present yourselves to God as being alive from the dead, and your members *as* instruments of righteousness to God. For sin shall not have dominion over you, for you not under the law but under grace." (Romans 6:13-14).

Christians are so fortunate to be "sons of God". We need have no thought for tomorrow: "For sufficient is the evil thereof". Let us live one day at a time. Further, we have no needs that are not already known by our Heavenly Father. It all comes down to: "Your will be done Father, not mine!" On our part we have to pray, receive, and give thanks in *"Now-Faith"*. But above all, we must implicitly *trust* the Holy Spirit and obey!

Assuming that we are addressing Christians in a steep learning-curve, let us turn to John 14:16-20.

"And I will pray the Father, and He will give you another Helper, that he may abide with you forever, the Spirit of truth, whom the world cannot receive, because it neither sees Him or knows Him; but you know Him, for He dwells with you and will be in you. I will not leave you orphans, I will come to you. At that day you will know that I am in the Father, and you in Me, and I in you."

As sons of God, authentic Christians are truly powered from within. This is what is meant by being indwelt by Spirit. How much more power do we need? Indeed, what are we waiting for?

Let us recall that we are not our bodies. We are an entity living within the body, and this entity will depart at an appointed time. Our body is the living temple of God.

When we have cleared our house of all darkness, we are "Children of Light". Both the Father and our Lord Jesus Christ shall live within us. Indeed, the Kingdom of Heaven is within us too! What a gift to be indwelt by the Trinity!

"Why gaze ye into the skies Steven, O wilderness warrior?"

"We was like ... lookin' for Him like ... far off ... but He ain't like, up in the sky. He's like inside us ... don't that beat all!"

"Steven! That which may appear to be boring Bible study can be downright fun! All we have to do is to delight in the Word of God, trust in God, and commit ourselves to a wonderful life journey."

The Christian odyssey however, will surely be filled with challenges. We will be assailed with situations involving life and death, family tragedies, hunger, despair, war, and financial woes.

This is the gift of *tempering*. It is necessary and it makes us stronger. It is essential for strong Christian growth. An extreme example of tempering can be seen in trees and plants that face up to strong prevailing winds. Note the acute angle at which they have grown and survived.

How many times do we have to be knocked down in life as we go our own wilful ways, before we wake up? Why do we, and others around us, rely solely on ourselves? Just who are we, so filled with busyness and self-centredness? This is a sobering question. We need to stop in our tracks and ask: "What is life all about?"

Most people are usually about 85 percent self-centred. We work, we struggle, we fight, we are unforgiving, we offend, we gossip, we judge, and condemn. This is usually based on *our* view of how things should be, or how we would like them to be.

In doing so, we are often quite cruel, hurtful, thoughtless, spiteful and controlling. This is we as human beings? Not always. We may have one small problem though, an old English proverb says: "A blind man will not thank you for a looking-glass!"

However, we cannot deny what we really are, or have become. It is time to face up to the reality of ourselves. Our Lord already knows everything about us anyway. It needs action on our part to bring things into focus.

Denial will not prevail. This is a humbling experience. It may even bring some of us to an awakened state. The point is, why do we need to face up to ourselves? And if we should, where do we go from here? We may need to see our world *differently*.

Gazing intently at a world map for a few minutes, one can transpose the land masses to oceans, and the oceans to land. As the map oscillates between the two states, it reveals a stunningly different view of planet Earth. In a like manner, one can transpose his soul and spiritual states. The oscillations yield progressive insights to higher consciousness.

Let us now explore two kingdoms. Not those of the earth, but those that dwell within us. They are the Kingdom of God, which is referred to sixty-eight times in the New Testament, and the kingdom of Heaven which is referred to about thirty-two times. Often these terms are used interchangeably. Theologians and scholars have deep explanations of these two kingdoms and are divided in their interpretations.

We simply refer to the Kingdom of God as it relates to our earthly tenure, and that which we need to achieve while we are still in our bodies. We relate the Kingdom of Heaven to that which we trust we will encounter on our passing.

We read in Matthew 6:33: "But seek ye first the kingdom of God and his righteousness, and all these things shall be added to you."

Jesus was not only referring to our ever-present bodily needs of eating, being clothed and surviving; He was clearly introducing the Kingdom of God, as a state of spiritual "being" to be attained. Jesus is the sower, the Son of man. He it is that plants the seeds of the Spirit. Those who have the inner ears and eyes to perceive these truths, will gain entry to the kingdom of God, and later, enter the Kingdom of Heaven.

In Matthew 19:24, Jesus says: "And I say to you, it is easier for a camel to go through the eye of a needle, than for a rich man to enter into the kingdom of God."

He is saying that the rich who are heavily involved in self, and being a power unto themselves, will have extreme difficulty in achieving even the first spiritual steps toward the Kingdom of God, which we term "Stage One".

Jesus gave us insight into body versus spirit. Normally, most of us are locked into acceptance only of that which we experience with our five senses. This is revealed by our behaviour and actions. Throughout His parables, Jesus is always attempting to bring us to the awakening.

This "awakening" is confirmed by the action of being baptized. "In those days John the Baptist came preaching in the wilderness of Judea, and saying, 'Repent, for the kingdom of heaven is at hand!' For this is he who was spoken of by the prophet Isaiah." (Matthew 3:1-2).

We now come to Mark 12:32, Jesus is speaking to a scribe who says to Him after one of His discourses: "Well *said* Teacher. You have spoken the truth, for there is one God, and there is no other but He. 34: Now when Jesus saw he answered wisely, He said unto him, 'You are not far from the kingdom of God'."

It would appear from this, that the scribe was close to the kingdom of God, and may well have been at the highest spiritual level attainable on earth. On his departure, he will ascend to the Kingdom of Heaven, which we term Stage Two. It primarily pertains to that which occurs upon our so-called death. The Bible states in Hebrews 9:27: "It is appointed for men to die once, but after this the judgement."

We are instructed that both the Kingdom of God and the Kingdom of Heaven are within us. We see the kingdoms sequentially in that order. Both are spoken of as a power which must work in the heart of man.

Jesus also revealed the status of those who attained the kingdoms, and we get a hint of levels within them. In Matthew 11:11, Jesus says: "Truly I tell you, among those born of women has not risen anyone greater than John the Baptist; yet he who is *least* in the kingdom is *greater* than he."

These levels of the kingdoms can be related to keys. There is an ancient story that may shed light: "We dwell in a mansion of many rooms. We take possession of the key to the first room, and then we ascend through successive states of being, room by room, and key by key, to ever higher spiritual levels."

There is not the remotest possibility of anyone who has just left that first room, of ever being able to pass on to another person, the knowledge and spiritual growth he acquired there. We experience learning individually, and by degrees.

"Man's indwelt octaves of insight, are a series of diatonic degrees of comprehension. In the spiritual acquisition of these degrees, Man creates the celestial harmonics of 'star music'." (From the Lost Notebooks of Wiser-Mouse).

Within this beautiful Christian matrix of "keys" there is thrilling empowerment in Matthew 16:19: "And I will give to you the keys to the kingdom of heaven, and whatever you bind on earth will be bound in heaven, and whatever you loose on earth will be loosed in heaven."

That alone, is a stunning gift of grace accessible only through *Now-Faith*. "I will give you the keys", is an astounding statement! We are empowered to act! Let us not play at Christianity "like kids in a Sunday sand-box!" Our acquisition of these keys, which include spiritual authority, belief, faith, salvation and prayer, are gifted us as we mature within Christianity.

Our Christian assemblies usually have only vague concepts of heaven involving angels, harps, and streets of gold, and we wearing crowns that we earned while here on earth. Having arrived in the kingdom of heaven, the common understanding is that we do nothing more but live in a state of bliss forever. Do all things come to a halt?

We are created in the image of God. We are the Spiritual sons of God. Let us therefore be assured, that we will not stagnate in a static pool of love. Neither God nor love is static.

"There is no break in cosmic continuity. God, Man, time and the aeons are integral with the flow of God's universal design." (From the Lost Notebooks of Wiser-Mouse).

We need to understand that Man, and certainly Time-man, is both intellectually and emotionally blind to the idea of the kingdom of God, or the kingdom of heaven. When Jesus preached that the kingdom of heaven *is at hand*, he did not mean that it is somewhere else. It means *here* and *now*. It calls for renewal!

We reiterate, the first step in our renewal is that of being born again. It must be understood as a spiritual process and not as an intellectual one. This re-birth embraces the concept of metanoia, which is genuine repentance or complete change of mind and direction.

We learn from Maurice Nicol that repentance in the Greek is "metanoia" which means change of mind. However, the English word "repentance" is derived from the Latin "poenitare" which means to feel sorry.

The Greek word metanoia has quite a different meaning that is not related to sorrow, mood or pain. It refers to a new mind, not a new heart. It is impossible to have a new heart, without possessing a new mind.

In Luke 13:3, Jesus said: "I tell you, no, but unless you repent you will all likewise perish." This is powerful! Christ says that unless a man repents he is useless and suffers a common fate, permanent death.

These are no idle words from Jesus. Let us not bury our Lord's words under an erroneous common human assumption. That is, regardless of our overt gross disobedience to God's Word, He will us love anyway, and accept us into the kingdom.

This belief emanates from pseudo-Christianity, and the "un-awakened". The cutting-edge of our misguided reality is that disobedience negates entry to the kingdom. We need to shoulder our responsibility.

Maurice Nicol says: "Man may sorrow but not to the point of metanoia. There is a special kind of suffering that leads to this, and it is of this type of suffering that Paul speaks when he contrasts it with ordinary suffering in life: 'For godly sorrow produces repentance *leading* to salvation, not to be regretted; but the sorrow of the world produces death'." (11 Corinthians 7:10).

We need to also examine Matthew 5:3: "Blessed *are* the poor in Spirit, For theirs is the kingdom of heaven." *Poor in spirit* means that we may possess nothing, and are utterly bankrupt of worldly things including food and shelter. We rely totally on God minute by minute throughout the day. This is the vehicle of faith whereby we live *in* the world, but not *of* it. We are God-sustained. At the apex of our journey, we shall dwell in both the earthly and spiritual dimensions.

"Living in faith is Man's act of receiving. It is prayer in motion, powered by trust." (From the Lost Notebooks of Wiser-Mouse).

An authentic Christian does not have to seek God. His relationship with Him is unbroken, through Jesus' sacrifice on the cross. However, it is not easy to be an authentic Christian. Veiled or open rejection and ridicule of the Word are common. Indeed, "And a man's enemies will be those of his own household." (Matthew 10:36).

"Blessed are they who are persecuted for righteousness' sake: for theirs is the kingdom of heaven." (Matthew 5:10).

"Whosoever therefore shall break or does away with, or relaxes one of the least important of these commandments and teaches men so, shall be called the *least* important in the kingdom of heaven, but he who practices them and teaches others to do so shall be called *great* in the kingdom of heaven." (Matthew 5:19).

From this it would appear that there are levels of attainment within the kingdoms. There is also a matter of basic qualification, and certain exclusions. [This is no wimpy push-over deal]. We need to understand the doctrine and teachings of Christ. Every day, we need to actually live the Word of God, not just read or hear about it on Sundays.

Jesus goes on to say that unless our righteousness exceeds the righteousness of the scribes and Pharisees, we shall in no case enter the kingdom of heaven. Christ is referring to man-made religions that embrace tradition, ritualistic rites and formalism, all of which are the children of hypocrisy. This is an exclusion.

What? Are we not *all* saved automatically through belief? Apparently not, for many are excluded from the kingdom of heaven.

Here is another exclusion. In Matthew 8:11, "Jesus said: 'And I say to you that many shall come from the east and west, and sit down with Abraham, Isaac, and Jacob in the kingdom of heaven. 12: But the sons of the kingdom will be cast out into outer darkness. There will be weeping and gnashing of teeth'."

In verse twelve where the "children of the kingdom are cast into outer darkness", one has to study the in-depth historical Biblical context to fully understand this exclusion.

In looking at exclusions, and no admittance signs, that bar us from the kingdom of heaven, one of them is "preparedness". We read in Matthew 25.13: "Watch therefore, for you know neither the day nor the hour in which the Son of man is coming." The whole key to being fully prepared for the day of Christ's return is contained in Jesus' parable of the wise and foolish virgins contained in Matthew 25:1-11.

Jesus is referred to in this parable as the "bridegroom", who is arriving at an unknown time to celebrate the marriage feast. His "bride" is the Christian church made up of Christians, referred to as "virgins".

Five of them are said to be prudent and *wise,* and five are said to be *foolish.* These ten virgins are thought by some to include Christians and non-Christians who seek to join Christ in the marriage banquet. We will regard the ten virgins as only those in some spiritual state already within Christianity. However, it appears that many, even "saved Christians", will not be invited to the marriage feast.

"And at midnight a cry was *heard*: Behold, the bridegroom is coming; go out to meet him!" (Matthew 25:6). Thusly, the scene is now set for the drama of life and death.

Matthew 25:7: "Then all those virgins arose and trimmed their lamps. 8: And the foolish said to the wise, 'Give us *some* of your oil; for our lamps are going out'. 9: But the wise answered, saying, 'No, lest there should not be enough for us and you; but go rather to those who sell, and buy for yourselves'."

10: And while they went to buy, the bridegroom came, and those who were ready went in with him to the wedding; and the door was shut. 11: Afterward the other virgins came also, saying, 'Lord, Lord, open to us!' 12: But He answered and said, 'Assuredly, I say to you, I do not know you'." (Reality has arrived).

Christians are the virgins awaiting the bridegroom. Some are wise, and have diligently prepared for the Master's coming. They have grown in grace. They are skilled in the flow-process of faith, and have experienced the power of prayer. They are committed to Christ, and since salvation, have only occasionally departed from the truth. If they were away for a while, like prodigals, they returned to continue their journey toward perfection. A spiritual state of preparedness prevailed.

The foolish virgins knew the Lord was coming, but were not prepared, even though they were already saved. Sometime after salvation, they became complacent, and thoughtlessly followed their own life-styles; or some man-made church that worships tradition. They slumbered. "It" was done for them without continuous effort on their part. It was their choice not to diligently prepare themselves for the unknown day.

At the start of this parable, all ten virgins have oil in their lamps. [Possession of oil illustrates the concept of being prepared]. As *born again* Christians, all of them also started out filled with the Holy Spirit. It appears that all the lamps were lit, but the foolish one's lamps were burning out. They had not provided against contingencies, in this case, the late arrival of the bridegroom. Our preparedness may apply either to Christ's second coming, some other mishap, or even to our own totally unexpected departure. The unprepared do not receive a second chance.

Those who receive Christ at the end of life will have no time left to prepare. A seed is received, but has no time to germinate, grow and yield fruit.

This tells us that we have to keep our lamps full. [Be constantly prepared]. This is achieved by walking in the Spirit and obeying His voice. This necessitates the engrafting of the Word in our hearts. We do not just start out one day, receive salvation, start going to church, and that is it! *Christians live Christianity.*

One cannot help but foresee some pseudo-Christians of today, charging those who had extra oil, [those who were prepared], with being selfish and unchristian, for not helping those in need. Do we allow lenience for those who are not *prepared* for events that must occur? Were they not forewarned? When and where is the line drawn, and by whom? When will we be ready?

Jesus' parable of the wise and foolish virgins clearly exposes a dangerous attitude of assumed entitlement on the part of many Christians. The apparent self-righteous mindset of these persons is: "Jesus loves us regardless of our disobedience. We are covered by His love. We are saved, we are always forgiven, so entry to the kingdom will not be denied us." (We will need to search ourselves on this quest with the aid of prayer, and the guidance of the Holy Spirit).

When the unprepared ones face their next disastrous scenario, will true Christians have the guts and power to say: "No! Go out and buy some! [e.g.oil]. We are prepared, why are you not prepared? On what grounds do we have to bail you out?" (Note that the wise ones in the parable would not yield to the request of the unprepared to "Help us!").

"Steven, you have that Eureka! 'I have found it' look on your face!"

"Like ... I was thinkin' of them virgins like ... you think we gotta like ... wise up too? No one like is gonna give them virgins ... or us ... oil like ... at that time of night. The doors is like ... locked man ... and they dumb virgins is like S.O.L." (So out of luck).

"Well said Steven! O like, valiant warrior! Remember that people remain ignorant, because they mistakenly feel they already know what is what, and that's a big problem."

"Man often believes and acts on that which he has incorrectly comprehended. Therefore, devoid of true understanding, he dwells in a trance-like state of unawareness." (From the Lost Notebooks of Wiser-Mouse).

In exploring these exclusions for entry to the kingdom, one again notes that when misfortune strikes, the unwise virgins' excuse is of the genre: "But we didn't know it was going to happen!" [e.g. If he knew he was going to die, he'd have bought some life insurance!]. It's all about those who are *not* prepared, for whatever reason they might haply bring to mind. *What did Jesus say?*

Jesus' parable clearly identified this pseudo-Christian state of unpreparedness. He took a firm stand, and established order and precedence. It was difficult for the late-comers to the marriage feast to accept Jesus' statement: *"I do not know you."*

This may well sound like "shock therapy" to some, but it is strictly scriptural. Also in Matthew 7:22, Jesus says: "Many will say to Me in that day, Lord, Lord, have we not prophesied in Your name, cast out demons in Your name, and done many wonders in Your name? 23: And then I will declare to them, I never knew you; depart from Me you who practice lawlessness!"

Many are going to appear before the Lord in that day, who sought to enter at the straight gate through a false intimate association with the Lord. They will perform works supposedly in the Lord's name, and in that day it will reveal that Jesus had nothing to do with these works.

In our acquisition of critical knowledge, we observe that no modern airline pilot flies an enormous Boeing aircraft, without first having excellence in training, through which he attains ultimate control. How can Christians who do not know their Bible, assume that they have the same level of training and experience in Christian practise, as those pilots have in flying their jets?

Indeed, one wonders how we would feel right now, if our Boeing pilot had a mindset of: "I don't have to go through the checklist; I took a course at one time." That would be unacceptable. By the same token, do we Christians understand that we shall have to attain a great deal of spiritual growth before we become mature Christians?

It would seem that we are making a series of critical judgements involving preparedness, our state of spirituality, and qualifications to enter the kingdoms. In view of this, let us briefly refocus on the subject of "objective criticism".

It is not of one individual criticizing or judging another. Objective criticism is simply a spiritual scriptural function of the mature Christian.

It could never be rebellion against the authority of God. In 1 Corinthians 2:15, it is said: "But he who is spiritual judges all things, yet he himself is *rightly* judged of no one."

Natural-soul-man is not involved in judgement. It is *Spiritual-man* who is in control. He is obeying the promptings of the Holy Spirit. It is the Holy Spirit speaking through the Christian that makes judgements and introduces change. It is through the mind of Christ. Not the mind of man.

On that note of wisdom, let us continue to seek knowledge to enable us to enter the kingdoms of God and of heaven. We need to refocus our comprehension on Jesus' beautiful "parable of the sower".

In so doing, we remove a lot of mystery, and discover why Mankind falls into two categories; those who believe, and those who do not believe. In Matthew 13:3, it is written that He spoke to the people of many things in parables saying: "Behold, a sower went out to sow."

Jesus continues His parable with a series of analogies comparing the Word of God to "seeds". These seeds are broadcast upon the Earth's surface by the Son of Man, our Lord Jesus Christ. They fall upon varying types of growing conditions. The "soil" into which these seeds are sown is the "mind" of Mankind. There is *natural-man* in whom the seeds may, or may not germinate; and there is *spiritual-man*, where high receptivity will enable the seed to take root.

It is here where we identify the "living dead", and those who are alive and spiritually awakened. We see that some seeds are immediately eaten by the birds, [the evil one]. Others fall on hot, inhospitable rocky soil; still others are choked by thorns, or some other catastrophe. Finally, there are those seeds that fall on good fertile soil. This is high yielding *spiritual-man*. He produces much "fruit".

We also need to bear in mind, John 3:27: "A man can receive nothing unless it has been given to him from heaven."

It is written in Matthew 13:10: "And the disciples came and said to Him, 'Why do You speak to them in parables?' 13:11: He answered and said to them, 'Because it has been given to you to know the mysteries of the kingdom of heaven, but to them it has not been given'.

13:12. "'For whoever has, to him will more be given, and he will have abundance; but whoever does not have, even what he has will be taken away from him'."

"Another parable He put forth to them, saying: 'The kingdom of heaven is like a man who sowed good seed in his field, but while men slept, his enemy came and sowed tares among the wheat and went his way. The servants of the owner came to him and told him what they had found, asking if they should weed them out'."

Jesus said: "Let them grow together until the harvest, and at the time of harvest I will say to the reapers, First gather together the tares and bind them in bundles to burn them, but gather up the wheat in my barn." (Matthew 13:30).

In the parable of the dragnet, Jesus says: "Again, the kingdom of heaven is like a dragnet that was cast into the sea and gathered some of every kind, which when it was full, they drew to shore; and they sat down and gathered the good into the vessels, but threw the bad away. So it will be at the end of the age." (Matthew 13:47).

"Therefore, every scribe instructed concerning the kingdom of heaven is like a householder who brings out of his treasure *things* new and old." (Matthew 13:52).

In Matthew 23:13, Jesus' words are: "But woe to you, scribes and Pharisees, hypocrites! For you shut up the kingdom of heaven against men; for you neither go in *yourselves*, nor do you allow those who are entering to go in."

This clearly defines the pathway to the kingdom of heaven and Eternity. Those who do not acknowledge that Jesus Christ is their shepherd are obviously lost sheep. They possibly belong to some other shepherd who is not connected with authentic Christianity.

In the kingdom, we will continue to worship God. Our lives will be, as we learned on our way to the kingdom; an eternal *now* of living prayer. In thanks, and obedience, we will carry out the will of God in a state of unspeakable joy and ecstasy.

We shall also live in our new spiritual bodies, whereby we will never again experience fatigue. "But those who wait on the Lord Shall renew their strength; They shall mount up with wings like eagles, They shall run and not be weary, They shall walk and not faint." (Isaiah 40:31).

At this point one cannot help but state: "Only rarely have we ever heard anything about the specifics of *instruction* and training for the kingdom of heaven from our Christian leaders".

The failure or omission of our leaders not to teach about this much neglected matter of the kingdoms, or numerous other spiritual imperatives, is a sin. "Therefore, to him who knows to do good and does not do *it*, to him it is sin." (James 4:17).

Upon spiritual due diligence and reflection, it would appear that our text consistently, "lays the heavies" on our church leaders. It may be recalled from our first and second chapters, that we are seeking to shed some light on this most primary of Christian spiritual questions:

"If the Christian teaching and practise in our churches is so right, what makes Christians of today so ineffective, so impotent, and so utterly powerless in the face of all the spiritual principles that Jesus taught?"

Are we really speaking of lack of organization in Christian instruction? Are the Christian spiritual objectives that we need to attain, merely left to the happenstance of the

Sunday morning message? Where is the strategic and tactical planning, the direction and purpose of spiritual enlightenment?

Christian shepherds may need to question their entire method of raising sheep, from lambing to maturity. The results, the spiritual evidence with which they are currently confronted, are precisely that which they have sown.

We Christians are experiencing the symptoms of a greater underlying problem. We need to face up to reality. The lack of spiritual progress in our churches can only be the direct result of *not* following the Scriptures.

This brings us full circle back to the regular Sunday church services. We have greetings and socializing, followed by worship in the form of music, a Bible message and prayers, after which we have fellowship with coffee and goodies, and we all go home for another week!

"Man un-awakened is incomplete. He sleeps. Sleep and death are 'time-states of oblivion' that do not exist in eternity." (From the Lost Notebooks of Wiser-Mouse).

However there is hope! We recall a certain man in Luke 13:6, who had planted a fig tree, and in due season it had produced no fruit.

The owner said to his worker: "Look, for three years I have come seeking fruit on this fig tree and find none. Cut it down; why does it use up the ground? But he answered and said to him, 'Sir, let it alone this year also, until I dig around it and fertilize *it*. And if it bears fruit, *well*. But if not, after that it can be cut down'."

This is an important message for us. To paraphrase the Bible, shape up, show positive intent and results or you'll be cut down. Some of us do not believe this. We are sure that our Lord Jesus is going to surround us with love, regardless of our wilful disobedience and excuses. ("I know you not!").

The parables of Jesus always picture the life-line still being open through metanoia, (repentance). But the message is crystal clear, repent, [have a change of mind or die]. We are instructed quite clearly, to be obedient to God's Word in the Holy Scriptures, or suffer the consequences. It is always we as individuals who elect to perish or not. Our free-will choices may cause us to abdicate our ascension to eternal life.

In Luke 13:4, Jesus was commenting on a construction accident where eighteen men were killed when the tower in Soloam fell and killed them. He said: "Do you think they were worse sinners than all *other* men who dwelt in Jerusalem? 5: I tell you, no, but unless you repent you will all likewise perish." (Note the tower falling and killing the workers had nothing to do with the common God's punishment human-label of judgement).

There are of course, many who either lack concern, or do not care. It probably means that they are not one of Jesus' sheep. But know this; if Jesus' words reach us and take root, we need to get proper Christian instruction, and refer to the Holy Bible as our authority.

There comes a time it is hoped when all of us may come to our senses. We need to equip ourselves for our journey to eternity. The Prodigal Son came to his senses after leading a destructive life-style, and we too have this same opportunity. We may come to, or return to our heavenly Father.

Basically, a man has one of two futures; one as Time-man in passing time, or the other as *Now-Man* in a changed state. Time will not bring about metanoia because we are always under the illusion that tomorrow will be different. It will not. That changed state is the result of humility and high self-esteem; but, high self-esteem should not be confused with being self-centred.

We reiterate that if and when Time-man completes his metamorphosis into *Now-Man*, he will eventually realize that this is where he feels more at home. He may be approaching the Presence of God.

Now-Man already knows definitively that death is *not*. God's plan for him was made before ever the foundations of the earth were laid. When he attains the state of being we know as, "I AM". He then has achieved oneness with the Father.

There is nothing Time-man can do within Levels One, Two or Three to change his past, other than to turn to our Lord Jesus Christ. Those recordings from his world of sin and sinful acts are then deleted from the record. Jesus said: "Though your sins be as scarlet, they shall be white as snow." He meant just that.

Jesus wipes the slate clean, provided that we accept His gift of forgiveness without reserve. We must search ourselves as we come before Christ. Are we retaining anything out of our past requiring forgiveness? If so, we are not clean.

All men need to let go of sin, otherwise it is slowly killing them in spirit, soul and body. Man was not designed to suffer, that is, to bear his cross as an act of unchristian fatalism. He was designed to grow spiritually and eventually be part of the household of God.

However, even *Now-Man* is still not perfect. While he physically inhabits the time dimension, he will continue to be guilty of yielding to sin, that is, doing other than the will of God.

Now-Man is yet typically human and fallible, although he has achieved access to great spiritual strength. He will always have to return to the foot of the cross for cleansing. That is, until he leaves his earthly form and the human time-frame.

Now-Man's state of awareness is closely linked to the Presence of God. He experiences unspeakable awe, great reverence, obedience and respect. He is aware that he is in the presence of his creator, who knows every thought he ever had, or ever will conceive. This knowledge in itself creates a foundation for walking in humility. God honours the humble.

"Man's heightened state of awareness and authority equates with his ever-increasing accountability to the Father." (From the Lost Notebooks of Wiser-Mouse).

In our exploration of the universality of God, interestingly, British physicist David Bohm reports from his research, that there is an *invisible field* that holds all reality together; a field that possesses the property of knowing what is happening everywhere at once.

Is David Bohm speaking of Acts 17:28:? "In Him we move and live and have our being"; and unwittingly speaking of God's omnipresence? The paradoxical conclusion of which, is that something travelling at speeds infinitely faster than light, equates with being at rest. We are there before we leave!

That is the simultaneity of being, which we call omnipresence. Add to that the all-knowing ability to receive and process data in *Now* and we have the omniscient being, our Heavenly Father.

We are observer-participants in a participative world. This is also revealed in Quantum Theory. Nothing is static or fixed. The functioning of our spirituality provides the key to the fundamental nature of our individual reality. Two notable quantum physicists, John Wheeler and Eugene Wigner, propose that: "Human consciousness is the crucial missing link between the bizarre world of electrons, and everyday reality."

From the human to the Godly, the only conscious Being who was here at the beginning of things was the Word [Jesus]. John 1:1: "In the beginning was the Word and the word was with God, and the Word was God. 2: He was in the beginning with God. 3: All things were made through Him, and without him nothing was made."

God *spoke* the worlds into creation by projected thought from His grand design. Authentic Christians, through the Holy Spirit, are indeed observer-participants, inasmuch that through *Now-Faith*, they also, "Call those things which do not exist as though they did." (Romans 4:17). It is our basic design!

"The spiritual word of awakened Man is the instrument that achieves miracles in his mosaic of reality. The Father is thereby glorified." (From the Lost Notebooks of Wiser-Mouse).

St. Augustine, who has just come on the scene, says: "Miracles happen, not in opposition to Nature, but in opposition to what we *know* of Nature.

We may not have previously viewed our world as the manifestations of our uncontrolled tongues! We have been in subjection to confusion. We observe, experience, and accept our everyday unreal dream-world as our only reality. The master key to our spiritual world, created by our tongues, through obedience, is the engrafted Word of the Gatekeeper.

Danah Zohar in her excellent book, *The Quantum Self,* gives a beautiful scientific example, of the power capable of being generated by two or more in synchronicity. She says: "Imagine for example, a large number of electromagnetic compasses lying on a table in a shielded room. Because the room is shielded, the compass needles point in no particular direction. If the table is jiggled, they swing randomly in every direction.

But if the electromagnetic energy in each compass is increased, the needles begin to exert a pull on each other, and slowly they line up into a uniform pattern. At the point where the electromagnetic current becomes strong enough to outweigh the effect of jiggling the table, it would have the dramatic effect of making the needles all point in the same direction.

All the separate compasses would then behave as one super-compass. We would say that the compass needles have gone into a condensed phase. The most ordered form of a condensed phase possible is a Bose-Einstein condensate.

The crucial distinguishing feature of Bose-Einstein condensates; is that the many parts which go to make up an ordered system, not only behave as a whole, but they become whole. Their identities merge or overlap in such a way that they lose their individuality entirely." (Author: This has the familiar ring of: "The Father and I are one").

"When cell membranes vibrate sufficiently to pull themselves into a Bose-Einstein condensate, they are creating the most coherent form of order possible in Nature, the order of unbroken wholeness." (Author: This state is achieved through prayer).

Zohar then raises the question: "What type of neurobiological mechanism would be required to line up neurons, [or some constituent of them], in the way the compass needles of the example were lined up by their own magnetic fields? And is such a mechanism feasible?" (Author, quivering with insight … "Yes!").

The Holy Scriptures afford excellent examples of this fact. Christ sent forth his disciples in groups of two or more. This had the effect of multiplying their power. Where there are two, three or more "compass-disciples", we have disciples operating in the unity of a "live Bose-Einstein condensate".

Christ's disciples went into condensed phases. Their spiritual powers and identities merged with each other and the Holy Spirit. They too, overlapped in such a way that they lost their individual identities, and became "one".

This is exactly the same position in which we are today. Christ said in Matthew 18:19: "Again I say to you that if *two of you* shall agree on earth concerning anything that they ask, it will be done for them by my Father in heaven."

In prayer, we lose our egos and our sense of self, to become one with God through our Lord Jesus Christ. Since Jesus' earthly departure, we now have the Holy Spirit [the Comforter] to guide us.

Isaac Asimov said: "The saddest part of life right now is that science gathers knowledge faster than society gathers wisdom."

British physicist Brian Pippard, in a comment on spiritual matters, states that: "The true believer need not fear, his citadel is impregnable to scientific assault because it occupies territory which is closed to science".

Increasingly, the fields of science and physics are ghosting into the spiritual realm. However, there are still religionists who try to have the last word.

In *God and the Astronomers,* the astrophysicist Robert Jastrow wrote this final paragraph: "At this moment it seems as though science will never be able to raise the curtain on the mystery of creation. For the scientist who has lived by his 'faith in the power of reason', the story ends like a bad dream. He has scaled the mountains of ignorance, he is about to conquer the highest peak; as he pulls himself over the final rock, he is greeted by a band of theologians who have been sitting there for centuries."

(The word theologians could be switched to read authentic Christians!).

Those who truly work in the spiritual dimension, acknowledge with gratefulness and admiration, the steadfast dedication of our scientists. Without their research, their scientific discoveries, and the application of those findings, there is no doubt that millions of us, including the author, would not be alive today.

There is also little doubt that a brilliant scientist like Francis S. Collins in his book *The Language of God,* opened many doors of understanding. His work on the human genome involving the cataloguing of the DNA of our species, with the hereditary code of life, is simple proof that scientists who work from facts, and those who work in the spiritual world, are a lot closer than they normally believe.

"Steven, you look confused!"

"Like man ... all this stuff ... blows my mind like ... so I don't know, what to think. I'm like ... up that famous creek ... an' I sure don't have no paddle!"

215

"How right you are! Fear not O like Holy Warrior, your Bible is the best paddle like you'll ever get! Remember what Tennyson wrote: 'Knowledge comes, but wisdom lingers'."

This brings us full circle to our Lord Jesus' wonderful simplicity. He spoke in parables. Jesus' messages are of astounding clarity. We too, must follow the rule of simplicity. All great truths are simple!

"Only Man committed by Christian baptism will mature into 'Christhood'. It is a life-long spiritual journey." (From the Lost Notebooks of Wiser-Mouse).

CHAPTER EIGHT

There are still those among us who *sleep* and are blinded by the evil one. That is, they cannot see or hear. "Whose minds the god of this age has blinded, who do not believe, lest the light of the gospel of the glory of Christ, who is the image of God, should shine on them." (2 Corinthians 4:4).

Satan is also called the "prince of the power of the air" Ephesians 2:2, and in John 12:31, he is called the "ruler of this world". This is not to say he rules the world completely. God does. It means that God has permitted Satan to operate, within the parameters He has allowed for Satan's agenda. God is in ultimate control.

Unbelievers are in bondage to Satan. He is the major influence in the minds of the majority of people. Satan's influence encompasses the goals, life-styles, false religions, commerce, philosophies, and most matters that govern our daily lives. Particularly, he generates the poison which issues from our tongues in prophecies of a negative nature. From this, we will understand that Satan is quite an adversary. This matter cannot be taken too lightly.

Believers are no longer under the rule of Satan. We read in Colossians 1:13, that: "He has delivered us from the powers of darkness and conveyed *us* into the kingdom of the Son of His love, 14: in whom we have redemption through His blood, the forgiveness of sins."

There are also those who have awakened but have split loyalties. They are warned in 1 Corinthians 10:21, "You cannot drink the cup of the Lord, and the cup of demons;

you cannot partake of the Lord's Table and of the table of demons." We need to commit to an irrevocable decision. (Are you for Me or against Me?)

Satan opposes God and God's Kingdom. Before his fall Satan was named Lucifer, son of the morning. It means bright and shining one. He was the "anointed cherub who covers". He would have been responsible for guarding the throne of God.

God created all spiritual beings, including angels, cherubim and seraphim. These three types of beings appear in the Bible. Each of them has a specific function. We only refer to angels in our treatise, and Satan was an angel with the seal of perfection. He was full of wisdom and perfect beauty.

We reiterate, that although God has His master plan, right now our planet Earth is primarily ruled by Satan and his powers of darkness. Some Christians are confused and upset about what kind of God we have, based on what we perceive in our world. We have wars, pestilence, famine, earthquakes and other disasters. Christians being in the middle of this conflict involving the *spirit of truth and the spirit of error* need to examine themselves. What do they have to discover, that holds them in bondage?

Our God is the God of the living, not of death and destruction. As Christians, we live *in* the world, but are not *of* the world. When Jesus returns to Earth with all His might and glory, Earth will again be fully governed by God. God's current access to us on Earth is through our contacting Him and asking.

"Be still, and know that I *am* God: I will be exalted among the nations, I will be exalted in the earth". (Psalm 46:10).

We learn from our Bibles that what is in store for us is of a magnitude far beyond our imagination to envision. "For then there will be great tribulation, such as has not been since the beginning of the world until this time, no, nor ever shall be." (Matthew 24:21).

It is difficult for us to envision the degree of terror and death in the event of nuclear war. Maybe this is the destruction that "lays waste at noonday" mentioned in Daniel.

"Therefore when you shall see the *abomination of desolation,* spoken of by Daniel the prophet, standing in the holy place. (Whoever reads this, let him understand)." (Matthew 24:15).

Enough said. That holy place must be our spiritual selves. We may lose our bodies, but our souls and spirits will survive.

Jesus said in Luke 10:18: "I saw Satan fall like lightning from heaven. 19: Behold, I give you the authority to trample on serpents and scorpions, and over all the power of the enemy, and nothing shall by any means hurt you."

We read in Ephesians 6:12: "For we wrestle *not* against flesh and blood, but against principalities, against powers, against the rulers of darkness of this world, against spiritual wickedness in high places."

Woe unto we who are not dwelling in the secret place of the most High God, or are separated from our Lord Jesus Christ. Without Him, we have no power to overcome the forces of evil.

[Jesus] "You are Peter, on this rock I will build my church, and the gates of Hades shall not prevail against it." (Matthew 16:18).

Whereas God is omnipresent, Satan is limited in location. Therefore he has lots of helpers. These are the demons and evil spirits. They are as much among us today as of yesteryear. It behoves every Christian to recognize that one of the *first* things Christ did, was to give His disciples authority over unclean spirits. (Matthew 10:1).

Graham and Shirley Powell in their penetrating work, *Christian Set Yourself Free,* explain that demons are living, intelligent but disembodied beings. Every spirit has a name and knows its function. Evil spirits are either inside of us or outside of us. If they are inside they have to be cast out. If they are on the outside, they have to be *kept* out.

The casting out of demons is as valid today, as it was in the time of Jesus. Most churches have never cast out demons and are silent on the subject. We should not become involved with evil spirits without guidance and instruction from the Holy Spirit. To achieve this, we need to link-up with authentic, mature Christian assemblies that are scripturally-based.

Masses of people came to Jesus for healing of their diseases, and casting out of demons.

Evil spirits have various powers and strengths. On one occasion the disciples came back to Jesus when they had failed to cast out a spirit. Jesus said it was mainly due to the disciples' lack of faith.

But, He added in Matthew 17:21: "However, this kind does not go out except by prayer and fasting." Thereby Jesus indicates there are different kinds of spirits with varying degrees of power. Only in the power of the shed blood of our Lord Jesus Christ shall we be enabled to overcome the works of darkness.

Subjection of the body to the Spirit ensures that *self* is under conscious control. Fasting and prayer are the primary requisites that empower us to follow Jesus' examples of casting out evil spirits.

It is imperative for us to recognize that fasting is evidence of self-control. To what have we been negatively yielding? If we cannot control our bodily selves, we lack spiritual power to resist evil. Some people live to eat, others eat to live. The body must be in complete subjection to the Spirit. Otherwise, we are acting against the will of God. We have become a power unto ourselves, which is negation of intent.

"What's that Steven?"

"Like ... like ... these evil spirits ... are real scary stuff like. I don't wanna' to be under their power ... like ..."

"Steven, it's worth making a study of the casting out of demons by focussing on Jesus' actions and commentaries."

We now need to examine how we are so directly responsible for our spiritual, mental and physical health. We always look outside of ourselves for help and healing. Let us explore how we may have become sick in the first place".

The time shall come, when we will look *within* to resolve whatever problems we are facing. We will openly declare before God and man, that it is we who have been playing host to negative sin elements. With our permission these are living within us, and slowly destroying us. We let them in. We hosted them. Sin grows cumulatively in the same way that a strangling vine in the jungle kills the host tree. Sin will kill our physical bodies, minds and spirits thereby preventing our entry to the kingdom of heaven.

Sin, is that which prevents us from not living abundantly in accord with the will of God. This means we've been "doing our own thing". Jesus said in John 15:5: "I am the vine, you are the branches. He who abides in Me, and I in him, bears much fruit; for without Me you can do nothing."

So, despite this crystal clear statement, we traipse off to follow our own wills and ignore our Creator. Most of us have no defined objective purpose in life; we dreamily drift, and endure from year to year, in the trance of the "living-dead".

We need to realize that our final spiritual metamorphosis is as miraculous as that of caterpillars bursting from their chrysalides. Figuratively, we too will burst forth in all magnificence as a wondrous winged-creature, taking flight within eternity.

However, our life focus, from the planting and reaping viewpoint, needs to be examined under the light of God. We expose ourselves, and our children, to continuous streams of negative images. People are not only fascinated by violence, blood-shed and terror, but embrace the concept that this is entertainment!

Indeed, murder is treated as an everyday occurrence, a game at which we play with great humour, as we endeavour to find out "whodunnit". This is evident both in our books, and in television programming. Some hotels even offer special weekend rates for "adventures in murder", and plot play-killings for us to solve. Murder is a game. Listen to our laughter as we find that the butler is really a good guy! Just what *is* this fascination with murder and violence for humans? Its power and insanity is surely of demonic origin.

Christians celebrating Halloween are also unwittingly giving recognition to demonic powers. Goblins, scary creatures, skeletons, evil faces, blood and terror and all that relates to horror are associated only with that which is satanic.

These Halloween celebrations have an aura of innocence, cuteness, and fun that originate in spiritual darkness. They bring confusion. Truth and error are intertwined. There is nothing in Halloween that relates to light, truth and the power of the living God.

Let us now examine some of the basic life elements in relation to where diseases come from, and how we play host to them. Nothing earth-shattering here, but we need to bring these thoughts into focus. There are a lot of provocative concepts "out there" to consider.

Our attention is directed to an astounding and somewhat disturbing fact. *It is that the brain's receptors willingly cooperate with the instructions we give to the mind!*

We have to very aware of the way we think. We can kill ourselves! Yes! The body obeys our commands whether we realize it or not. Our thinking can attract forms of sickness, or it can attract healing. The very fact that such matters can to some measure be controlled by us provides a wonderful sense of peace and well-being.

We think primarily with one-sided left-brain logic. We rarely draw upon the inputs from our right-brain. The truth is that we were designed to work in a whole-brain capacity. Traditionally, the human brain has been seen purely as a logic unit. Beyond this whole-brain approach, Edelman theorized quite a while ago: "That every experience changes the brain's anatomy."

We now have a concept called "neuroplasticity". This refers to the discovery that our brains have the ability to alter their structure. They do this in response to our experiences, and our reactions to them. This includes the brain's ability to survive and carry on after severe injury. Regardless of age, the brain is constantly forming new neural pathways, removing old ones, and changing the strength of existing connections.

A well-known saying about neuroplasticity is: "Neurons that fire together wire together, and neurons that fire apart wire apart." This simply means, that when neurons activate at the same time in response to a thought or event, they become associated with one another, and their connections become stronger.

This has the exponential effect of positively or negatively increasing their power. Our brains are primarily receiving organs, with the ability to amplify incoming messages. Sir John Eccles: "It is quite astonishing that with every thought; the mind manages to move atoms of hydrogen, carbon and oxygen and other particles in the brain's cells." Pure thought changes the brain's activity, its circuits, and very structure!

We need to apply Jesus' basic sowing and reaping principles to our electronic communication age. We perpetually program our minds from internet, and text messaging inputs, but to what end? Just what is it that we are planting? Dare we confront the reality of the crop or harvest? Christ's principles yield spiritual perspective.

We are spirit and soul entities, operating within a body. The purpose here in relating neuroplasticity to authentic Christian thinking, is to establish stronger communication lines with our heavenly Father.

When we Christians fully comprehend Awareness Level Four, and act in this dimension consistently, we will be building God-specific transmission lines in our brains. We will refer to these as *"T-Lines"*.

When we track game-trails in our forests, we observe that some are difficult to follow. Others are so well-travelled that we know they are main trails. So it is with the tracks, or T-Lines, in our brains. With their increased usage, we will achieve ever higher levels of spiritual power.

The key to the power of neuroplasticity is for us to focus sharply on consciously establishing our tracks or T-Lines. This is achieved through our Gatekeeper, which is He of the engrafted Word.

Our constant usage of Now-Faith, grace, forgiveness, and the gifts of the Holy Spirit, will yield effortless access to this spiritual highway. The brain will change its structure to accommodate our frequent travel on this specific track of thought-activity. Our thought processes become easier, almost the same as being on auto-pilot.

The fact that changes *do* take place, and we did it, consciously, or unconsciously, is all okay, unless it has its foundation in negativity. But let us beware, for we shall also see this same neuroplasticity concept and all that it entails, being offered by those who operate from their souls only. In the field of achieving success through positive thinking and reliance on ourselves, the master-counterfeiter has no peer in the art of deception

Some of our T-Lines will be running so deeply, that they will contact the very blueprint of our creation, which is the intelligence of our DNA. The term intelligence belongs to all four awareness levels. However, in Level Four we know, and knowing in this state is beyond both logic and linguistics.

Let us also recognize that many of us have not even considered things of this nature, and therefore, we may not yet be able to consciously trigger neuron-affinities to change our brain's anatomical structure.

We understand that scientists working from fact and logic, examined Einstein's brain to discover its secret genius. They did not succeed. From our unscientific naïve viewpoint, this is like us taking a television receiver apart to locate a famous symphony orchestra!

The Greek philosopher Heraclitus remarked, and it's an ancient thought, that: "One cannot step into the same river twice". This is because the river, [the brain and stream of consciousness], is constantly changing. New water, [thoughts] are continually rushing in. The conscious control of thoughts in this river of time is our responsibility. It shapes our lives!

In seeking physical and psychological health, we need to realize that we have an "interior intelligence". It is as if all the cells in our bodies are permeated with latent healing power. Our mature actions; under the direction of the Holy Spirit, would involve the conscious imaging and directing of this interior intelligence.

Correctly focussed, it would not concentrate on a specific organ, isolated condition, or malfunction; because it is not segregated of itself. This interior intelligence is not in separate parts. It is wholeness working with wholeness. Nothing is excluded or in isolation. It could be likened to an orchestra conductor, directing thousands of elements, to create a glorious whole.

In praying to our heavenly Father for health, we know that He is aware of our specific health problems. Were we to request the healing of one isolated part, we would be primarily requesting God to treat a symptom. Symptoms cannot survive the wisdom of God's scrutiny. God eliminates symptoms by identifying and correcting base problems.

Let us repeat; the brain's receptors willingly cooperate with the instructions God imparts to us through the Holy Spirit. The instructions that we do give, and that will be obeyed, are linked exactly to the level of comprehension that we have attained. We can employ positive thinking [soul] methods to our healing, or we can work with God's spiritual power. We become whole in the spiritual realm, through what we have termed *Now-Faith.*

Paul Tillich in his *Eternal Now*, says that a large part of Jesus' recorded healings were of three types. He comments: "Those in which people sick of body are directly healed; those in which people sick of body were forgiven and healed; and those in which people were sick of mind are delivered from what is called demonic possession."

Tillich continues: "It is regrettable that most preaching emphasizes the miraculous character of these stories, often using a poor, superstitious notion of miracles, instead of showing the profound insight they betray into disease, health and healing, the inseparable unity of body and mind."

We live primarily in a spiritual universe, with both evil and Godly powers at work. We are aware that fear can summon Satan and his demons on to any scenario. *Now-Faith* ensures that God is summoned to the scene. Our healing needs to penetrate the deepest levels within ourselves, where our spirits, minds, and our physical bodies meet. We need to take this seriously as it deeply involves Level Four, this, being a pivotal-shift-access-point.

The neuroplasticity we referred to, whether positive or negative, will immutably leave tracks in our physical bodies.

Once we have accepted a disease or ailment from whatever source, we are then hosting this dark element.

Having blueprinted them, our thoughts immediately move molecules within the brain according to our permitted acceptance limits. This will also reveal the specifications of our rejection limits. Will we reject some, or all of these negative disease factors?

A typical example is our accepting the fact that a cold will eventually go away. Whereas, were the diagnosis for a serious disease, whether curable or not, we tend imprint our acceptance, and arrange to *host* the intruder.

True, this is simplistic, but we have to consider *how* this alien was enabled to enter us in the first place. It had to originate from somewhere, because it is here. The Bible cites a number of cases of how, when, where and why disease and disability beset certain persons, and how they were cured. Christians need to be fully cognizant of all these cases.

A typical attitudinal concept is that anything goes. There is no control. A family member may say: "You're getting a cold, I can tell!" To which the "host" may reply: "I guess so, my throat is awfully rough too." Right there! *We* have given permission to this alien element to take up residence.

Alternatively, the victim-host may reply: "No! Definitely not! I am tired though, I'll get some extra rest." Here was an immediate statement of rejection. This caused the brain to move immune-defence molecules in line against the attack. This was our conscious defence, our intent. We are in control. In the final analysis *we* are responsible.

There is evidence that when *we* step in as the control-authority, we are able to overcome many of these oppressions with mental imagery. As well, there is evidence that this is effective in treating cancer and other diseases. It would take volumes to explore this. Firstly, let us spiritually banish any suggestion of being unwell.

Christians recognize: "To that which we yield, its servants we become". We have an invisible force-field of light emanating from us. We already know that darkness recedes or disappears when light approaches. We must clearly envision these dark spiritual elemental forms fleeing before us. We do not acknowledge their appearance in any form.

In prayer we reject and bind an illness or other challenge. We then thank our heavenly Father. In Now-Faith it is completed. Observe the pivotal-shift action here, which is not giving it a second thought. It is God's will, released. We left the matter at the foot of the Cross. Christ himself said: "It is finished." It is! This gift of grace is a spiritually-engineered craft of unsurpassed beauty for cruising all of eternity!

Our light within, powered by the Word in Now-Faith, will gift us the abundant life as Jesus promised. We need to obey the spiritual commands of our heavenly Father who is the Father of lights.

"Man as an authentic son of God is a Child of Light. No element of darkness can penetrate his spiritual raiment. No form of evil can exalt itself above "I AM", the one true God." (From the Lost Notebooks of Wiser-Mouse).

We have to remind ourselves that: "God is not mocked. That which a man sows, that shall he reap". We as individuals dictate our own reality. We are born of free will. We can obey or disobey. We may opt-out anytime we wish! However, there will be penalties!

Let us now take a peek at *stress.* It appears to be pandemic. The billions of dollars we invest in pain-killers and sleep-promoting drugs, [while ignoring their devastating side-effects], stress us out even more. If the pain doesn't kill us, the side-effects will!

We drop into bed at night really stressed-out, with the problems of *today* and *tomorrow.* That in itself is a terrible burden to carry. We may feel our problems are insurmountable. There is nowhere to turn. No one understands. It is as though we had isolated ourselves on an island of depression in an ocean of humanity. Why? Is it that we unconsciously persist in the belief that we are a "power unto ourselves?" Is it that we believe that it is only *we* who can solve our problems?

With this particular scenario in mind, let us tackle our insomnia-type, stress-related situations. These awaken us after the first few hours of sleep have taken the edge off our rest. We'll firstly, have to assume that no communication occurred between God and us, before we went to sleep.

That is not good, because it is now 2:00 AM. Often we toss and turn before exclaiming: "Not another of those nights. God! I'll go crazy". Pills are not the answer. Medications for sleep are "Band-Aid" solutions. Stress accumulates, and can produce bizarre health symptoms, of a very real nature. It cannot be dissipated unless *we* step in, by allowing God to take over!

When we acquire this change of mind, we will need to abandon the concept of: "I can take care of everything myself. God does not answer prayers anyway and I have the experience to prove it." Our current condition is exactly the result of what we have planted, and are now reaping. So this mistaken belief of: "I am a power unto myself", is a complete fallacy. (As they say in court, we rest our case).

"Steven, you look unsure of this, like you're inundated with doubts!"

"Like ... like man ... the way you stacks it all up like man ... it's like you is sayin' that we is all God, like. We ain't that perfect!"

"You are right on the nose about one thing Steve, we *are* God-like. We read in Psalm 82:6: "I said, You *are* gods, And all of you *are* children of the Most High.""

Let us pick up on this God-like comment. Yes! We are gods! But let us approach this with caution! Take a look at John 10:34: "Jesus answered them, 'Is it not written in your law, I said, You *are* gods? 35: If He called them gods, to whom the word of God came (and the Scripture cannot be broken').""

In this paragraph, Jesus was speaking of Himself. Our claim to being Gods is only: "For as many as are led by the Spirit of God, these are the sons of God." (Romans 8:14).

Authentic Christians possess Godly heritage, but they have not arrived at godhood. They are joint-heirs with our Lord Jesus Christ with baptism in the Holy Spirit.

Jesus' teachings, Jesus' death on the Cross, and His rising from the dead on the third day, contain the keys to heaven and hell. As spirit-led sons of God, the Holy Spirit is here right now. He will provide us guidance and instructions from the Father. Our duty is to recognize these incoming messages and to obey them.

We fully acknowledge Jesus as our Saviour, Intercessor, Son of God, Judge of all men and their works. We recognize that the Father has put all things into the hands of the Son.

Despite these powerful avenues of direction, many Christians are still trapped in the victim-mind-set. Namely, that we are poor creatures who have to bear our cross, and suffer mightily to win our crowns of glory.

These are falsehoods. Authentic Christians do not deny that they are sinners, but they do not adopt a permanent sin mindset by concentrating their thoughts on sin. They are not victims. Authentic Christians are the sons of God, not poor, beaten, down-trodden fearful sinners. (Some religious hymns need to be translated through the eyes of authentic Christianity).

Here is a beautiful message from *Johannes Metz,* in his *Poverty of Spirit.* He says: "Becoming a human involves more than conception and birth. It is a mandate and a mission, a command and a decision. A human being has an open-ended relationship to himself. He does not possess his being unchallenged; he cannot take his being for granted as God does his.

Man is challenged and questioned from the depths of his boundless spirit. 'Being' is entrusted to him as a summons, which he is to accept and consciously acknowledge.

He is never simply a being that is there and ready-made just for the asking. From the very start he is something that can be; a being who must win his selfhood and decide what he has to be. He must fully become what he is, a human being. To become man through the exercise of his freedom, that is the law of his Being.

Man must learn to accept himself in the painful experiment of his living. We must beware; man's flight from developing himself begins early. To become man, means to have no support and have no power. Only through poverty of spirit do men draw near to God; only through it, does God draw near to man. Our needs are always beyond our capacities, and we only find ourselves when we lose ourselves."

Humble acceptance of our authentic Being is self-love in the Christian sense. In biblical terms it is poverty of spirit. It is man bearing witness of himself professing loyalty to his radical poverty, and shouldering the weight of self-emptying. It is man's consent to self-surrender. Metz says: "In poverty of spirit man learns to accept himself as someone who does not belong to himself."

It is no accident that poverty of spirit is the first of Christ's beatitudes. Jesus said in Matthew 5:3, "Blessed *are* the poor in spirit, for theirs is the kingdom of heaven."

Throughout our treatise when we examined Now-Faith, moving mountains, and fervently praying, we have emphasized that we have to abdicate our throne of self. It is not we, but the Father within who doeth the works. Poverty of spirit is recognizing that we have no power of ourselves. We are merely the branches, He is the vine. (John 15:1).

We have touched on poverty of Spirit, and we recognize that everything that exists comes from God, and belongs to God. Everything we say we own is not really ours. We are merely stewards of our possessions. Stewards are caretakers, they manage, but they do not own. That includes our vehicles, our homes, our ATVs and electronics, and all our cash assets.

"What's that Steven?"

"Like ... we worked hard for this stuff ... an' all cash like too ... we ain't a bunch of 'scuffians' shootin' up drugs an' stuff like ..."

"That's true Steven. Let's pause for a moment. We are all stewards of our possessions for but a brief period of time.

Worse still, a lot of that high-priced stuff owns us, if we dare to admit to it!"

"Like ... you're sayin' my rifle an' my truck ... are like idols ... golden-calves like? I don't worship them, but I'm sure glad I'm a steward of them! But it sounds to me like, you gonna talk about tithin' and stuff. I know ... plantin' and reapin' ... most of us don't give ... like we ain't got no cash to plant because we gotta eat!"

"Noble Christian, dead-broke, Bambi-whackin' friend of the wilderness; I "been there and done that", there ain't nothin' new under the sun. I was young once."

Steven's comments triggered memories of early life challenges. I was always desperate for cash. Just like being newly-born I had nothing. The only reason I went to a church service, was because after one had suffered through the boring singing and praying stuff, they offered coffee, sandwiches and little cakes. I had so little to eat for so many days that I needed string to hold up my pants. A belt was unaffordable.

I was a "scruffian" back then, as were my dubious friends. We cleaned up in cafe washrooms, slept in "our" cars, and were opportunistic survivors. We felt that the real "me" inside each of us was a decent guy. That was our reality. We were just honest in our desperate attempts to live. We could find no way through our dilemmas.

I was once asked by a group of nice tea-sipping church ladies if I had found Jesus. I explained to them, my face a mask of wonderment and surprise, that I didn't know He was lost! They blushed, sputtered in their tea and took off. I belonged to a scruffy set of individuals that one would hesitate to trust.

True, we acquired a couple of cars illegally, and siphoned gas by night in order to run them. We then sold the excess gas to friends so that we could eat. Licence plates and registrations were alien to us in those days, and we had as wary an eye for cops as rabbits have for weasels.

Later, when I was on firmer but still Godless ground, although I did open the Bible sometimes, I found myself in a bank requesting a loan.

They were obviously non-Christian, because when the banker asked me for collateral against my loan, I boldly stated: "I have none, but my Father owns the cattle on ten thousand hills." My face was a vision of light, and quite *Holy*. "Well", said that banker, "You'd better go ask him for the loan then."

Around that time, a pastor told me that to have lots of cash you have to give it away! Plant it. I told him I had no seed money to plant. I was even desperate enough to suggest that he must be very rich in following that strategy. When he saw I was about to put the bite on him for some cash, he switched directions, and offered me a fresh coffee and an old stale donut. Despite this, my soul would not be saved yet.

At that same church one Sunday, when the collection plate came by, I actually tried, unsuccessfully, to *lift* a few bucks. [How can one ever forget the looks on the faces of those who observed my failed sleight-of-hand]. People gave it away, I needed it. It made sense to me! This was surely Christian generosity.

That cost me coffee and sandwiches, and I left that assembly for good. Couldn't they feel my hunger, see my need, hear my belly loudly rumbling, or see the desperation in my eyes? Or is that why they had that scared look when our eyes met?

At that time I was sleeping in "my" 1952 Buick Roadmaster; my home, my pride and joy. It was dead of winter and 42 degrees below zero Fahrenheit. I hid out under a highway overpass by a frozen creek. Both the sheriff and the finance company wanted that car and me in the worst way.

I felt like a hunted animal. I had to light a small fire under the oil-pan each morning to free up the oil, and at the same time try to avoid the whole shebang from exploding in flames. Having stolen some tea bags the previous day, I broke some ice out of the creek, lit a small fire, melted the ice and made tea in my hubcaps. (They were made of metal in those days).

When the "hot" car was serviced, the mechanics were mystified by the two front blackened hub-caps. I had to explain that one was my "saucepan" for boiling water for tea, and the other was a "frying pan", for when I lucky enough to catch a fish. I was up that famous creek. In 1952, as a result of a failed entrepreneurial fire extinguisher marketing scheme, I owed banks and other people some $20,000.00. At that time it was the equivalent of owning two medium-sized homes!

Steven said: "Hold it! Like ... like ... enough already yet! You was one poor S.O.B. an' the Christians like ... was so dumb and filled with their selves ... they like ... was too scared to help you!"

"I truly think you have it Steven, anyway we're right on track as we talk about *money!*"

This has landed us in the middle of some Christian financial concepts. (We've at least saved that which is possibly the most hurtful Christian topic till last).

There is this little thing called "tithing". Oh no! Oh yes! They want your money! (They always warned us about these money-grabbin' preachers, always got their hands out for your cash!).

Okay, we'll cool it and read 2 Corinthians 9:6: "But this I *say*, He who sows sparingly will also reap sparingly, and he who sows bountifully will also reap bountifully. 7: So let each one give as he purposes in his heart, not grudgingly, or of necessity; for God loves a cheerful giver."

"God's covenant with Man Is honoured by the act of tithing. It is spiritual stewardship of Man's total resources. Tithing is the evidence of faith expressed. It is an immutable living love-trust." (From the Lost Notebooks of Wiser-Mouse).

It will be recognized that we have returned to the planting and harvesting principle. This runs through everything we do in life in this earthly dimension. We plant acorns for oak trees, apple seeds for apple trees; it therefore flows as night into day, that one sows cash to reap cash.

If we say we have faith, yet have not tithed, we have robbed and defrauded God. Malachi 3:8: "Will a man rob God? Yet you have robbed Me! But you say, 'In what way have we robbed You?' In tithes and offerings. 9: 'You are cursed with a curse, For you have robbed Me, *even* this whole nation'." (Oh Wow! Man! That hurt!).

10: "Bring all the tithes into the storehouse, That there may be food in My house, And try Me now in this," says the Lord of hosts, "If I will not open for you the windows of heaven

And pour out for you *such* blessing That *there will* not *be room* enough *to receive it*."

It is a rule of thumb that about 10 percent of our net income is what we assign to growing the Church. Christians in their places of congregation have the same bills that householders have; rent or mortgage, heat, light, water, maintenance of the building and its facilities.

Surprise! Even the pastors ought to be paid, sometimes! We also need money for special kid's camps and projects. The Scriptures lay the "heavies" on us in this matter of tithing, and rightly so.

We claim we have faith in God? Tithing is an on-going reality which confirms this faith. When we give from the heart, [inconspicuously], seeking no reward, a wonderful, serene feeling overcomes us.

When we have tithed, we feel to be a part of everything. We belong. We have contributed. What love! The only side-effects are happiness and Eternal Life. We are primarily spiritual beings in development.

Those of us who are now Christians, may recall the many times we rejected the efforts of others who tried to introduce us to our Lord Jesus Christ.

One of only two poems that survived from the *Lost Notebooks of Wiser-Mouse* may shed some light. It appears to have been written early in the shepherd's spiritual journey.

> "A Christian dropped by the house one day,
> He spoke of Jesus and how to pray,
> Perceived I a zealot with much to say,
> So I dismissed him. He went his way.
>
> He'd looked fully at me, so gracious a smile,

My resistance faded for more than a while.
Then gone was that angel to spaces above,
He'd gifted me words filled with God's love."

Christians have a duty to bring more sheep into the fold. Those who possess mature spiritual knowledge are commanded to guide the new sheep. In attempting to fulfil this mission we may encounter rejection.

The question is why do we feel rejected? Why would we feel personal affront? Is it that we have fallen asleep? Are we putting forth our effort to achieve this? If so, we have not spent enough time in true prayer. We are going forth on His mission with *our egos;* not the Spirit of God.

Steven and I were far away in pure wilderness, and quite remote from the haunts of man. We had a beautiful hot fire waiting to cook our evening meal. I watched the flickering flames, and absorbed the heat as it coursed new life through my tired limbs. These same logs, were now releasing the stored scorching heat of a hundred or more past summer suns.

In the cool of the on-coming night-breeze, I stood in silent wonder. I thanked God for providing this much-needed heat. I was thoughtful for some moments, giving the *Wiser-Mouse Legacy* a break.

Steve finally blurted: "Like ... like ... you gonna give me some peace now? I was like ... feelin' ... I was a write off ... time you was done with me. Right now! I'm gonna like ... cook up some supper ... at the same time ... you can do some Bible thumpin' if you was of a mind—or whatever." He walked quickly away.

I sat on my log, stretched out and yawned, "Sounds good to me Steve", I contributed. Dusk was arriving with the first stars. Below us, was a swift-flowing river, alive with wishy-washy water music. The slap of diving salmon, mingled with the early call of owls, were the only sounds of night-magic that fell upon our ears.

Grizzly bears were feeding in the same river. Within more than a kilometre distance, every grizzly knows what type of creature we are, where we are, and in all probability they are also aware of our intent. We are harmless. Neither the grizzlies, nor we, are concerned with each other. Their search is for more fish to fatten up before winter hibernation.

My need and purpose at this time, is to exercise my spiritual wings, to empower them for flight. It is similar to a young eagle, flapping his pinions to gain strength and confidence before leaving the nest.

This is an exhilarating scenario, where one's entire yearning is a probing search, which is absorbed by the early star-lit heavens. One can almost take flight! The approaching night conveys multiple worlds of consciousness within, and beyond space-time. It is here that spiritual flight is experienced. In these dimensions, linguistics are unknown. The entire cosmos becomes "is" and "Now". Time is "not".

It is a strangely beautiful spiritual experience for a human to be merged with the wilderness, the wild creatures, and nighttime infinity. Time is neither a factor or measurable in this mindset.

However, earthly reality can swiftly return when the spirit yields to the physical, as must be, when the aroma of hot stew and freshly baked biscuits wafts across the clearing. In mystic wonder I returned to the fire.

Steve and I spoke little during supper. It was the silence of friends who do not have to speak. All is known. But while we sipped our coffee, I ventured a few comments.

"You know Steve, we are sown into the aeons in successive periods of time by the Son of Man. All of us are really in the same position as the Children of Israel, on their way to the Promised Land. You know, the 'land of milk and honey'.

Their experience was, and is, the same as our bitter complaints, rank debauchery, and the worshiping of idols. Further, they were also disobedient, and abandoned the spiritual leadership of those in charge."

"You", I stated, as Steve checked out and loaded both our rifles, "are in the earlier stages of 'departing from Egypt, fleeing from Herod' and the hell of his rule. It is an immense journey through almost trackless wilderness, on this most Holy Christian odyssey."

The entire biblical record of the people of Israel in their journey parallels our own allegorical-imperative. It's the journey we are born into, whether we like it or not! Of free will, we make our choices. Some will elect to return to Egypt. Some will die of starvation and other causes in the wilderness. Others will emerge beyond the wilderness and witness before them, the Promised Land. Moses was the Israelites' wilderness guide. They had to journey through the wilderness the same as we; to learn what we've been studying in this flight-path to eternity.

Steven then prepared to snug the camp down for the night. The key question was; have we missed anything that could cause us to change from being observers into becoming prey? We slept soundly, undisturbed. Right after early sunrise we checked for grizzly activity. All being well, we consumed a wonderful breakfast, and I returned to the creation of the *Wiser-Mouse Legacy*.

Man is his understanding of Time. In our lifetime we have progressed through a series of states of consciousness.

Now, some of us are experiencing the stirring-power of "spirit-wings". We are stronger now in spirit than we are of body. It feels so much more natural to be primarily self-possessed in the spirit.

It is a realization of, or a return to permanence. From that state one can view one's molecular body as being quite temporary in nature. It is as we said in the beginning, we have a body, but we are not our body. We are an entity that dwells within this Temple of the Holy Spirit.

"Obey my voice, and I will be your God, and you shall be my people." (Jeremiah 7:23). In absolute obedience, we will learn humility, and experience the fruits of obedience. To experience love under the guidance of the Holy Spirit, translates us from the state of being mere Time-man, into the Spiritual realm of *Now-Man*.

On one of our wilderness trips, Steven was introduced to one of the actual *Lost Notebooks of Wiser-Mouse.* Already, having been intrigued by the previous poem, his piqued curiosity knew no bounds as he very carefully turned the pages of a *Lost Notebook* to the second surviving poem.

Here is what Steven read aloud, among his chuckles:

Vapour Trails

"The fallacies of ego, are the fallacies of "self",
A dream-world of ignorance, of power and of pelf,
Ego is the sleep-state that infects the "living-dead",
They feed on illusions, like freshly-baked bread.

See yon tree-lined acres, stretching to the skies,
These are graveyards of souls, many will not rise,
While chiselled into stone are memories of those,
Whose after-life died as they laid in repose.

We're foggy trails of vapour, that's all we really are,
Elements molecular, blown from a distant star,
New grass pushing up through the fertile earth,
Only to be burned up by scorching sun from birth.

Self-importance yields a life of deadly pride,
Here today, gone tomorrow, just here for the ride,
Are we soul and body only, with no spirit life?
It is we who chose to dwell, where evil is so rife!

Some dwell eternally in the heaven-house of God,
While spiritless ones lie, lost beneath the sod,
Others took wings, left their bodies behind,
Possessing all eternity with Godly Spirit-mind."

(From the Lost Notebooks of Wiser-Mouse).

This poem could well have been based on:

Job 14:1: "Man that is born of woman is of few days, and full of trouble. 2: He cometh forth like a flower, and is cut down: he flees also as a shadow, and continues not."

Steven chortled. "Like ... I was readin' that poem ... it rhymes like and makes sense! That Wiser-Mouse guy ... is he really a mouse ... like? You sure he ain't really a guy?"

Avoiding a reply I said: "Speaking of mice, O questing one, did you ever hear a white-footed mouse sing? R. D. Lawrence did, he was a nature guy like us. He stayed in the wilderness for long periods of time, and allowed the whole wild-world around him to unfold."

Steven looked appraisingly at me with that half-apologetic, "I just gotta say this" expression that I knew so well. But before he could say anything, I continued with a burst of enthusiasm: "Steven, did you know that biologists have studied a number of singing mice? They exhibit two-octave ranges, and tempos varying from two to six notes per second? I'd just love to hear Wiser-Mouse sing!"

Steve gave his famous time-out signal. It really said: "Shut up", in a very nice way. Sometimes though, in desperation he sprinkled his demands of me with colourful expletives that he borrowed from his logging camp days.

"Like ... I'm feelin' ... you like ... an' me ... have had enough right now ... of this Bible stuff ... 'specially when you gets talkin' like ... 'bout mice and rabbits and stuff. Here! Grab a handful of this hot roast chicken an' stuff it in your pie hole!"

Yum! Yum! Roast chicken and potatoes right off red-hot rocks. "Supper sits really well with me O 'Bambi-Whacker'. I'm feeling real earthy tonight! It's dark, gettin' cold, and afore I chaws on this 'ere chicken, gimme me a couple of big swigs of that Grand Marnier stuff you've been totin' round. Thanks!" (Sometimes it feels so good to get back in touch with the crudeness of the earthly, and let the *natural-man* take over!).

The stars are super bright tonight. Wolves are howling, causing eerie feelings that cause the hairs on my neck to rise. It's also a sure bet there's a grizzly not too far away. We're in their territory, and there may be an upcoming visit.

However, we are prepared. We have our big-bore rifles with us, but it is rare for us to experience encounters of the unwelcome kind.

Despite this, there are times when darkness descends that we feel like the small creatures that we really are. The grizzly bear is indeed at the top of the food chain! Snuggled into our sleeping bags, we recognize human frailty. We automatically listen for strange noises too.

However before sleeping, the Holy Spirit gently overtakes us with prayer. This is when we are reminded that the Bible is God's gift to man. It is our foundation of trust. It is a living spiritual instrument. The Word of God "IS". Our Father gifted us a number of powerful unbreakable promises.

"Let not your heart be troubled, neither let it be afraid."

"I will never leave you or forsake you."

"Trust in the Lord with all your heart."

"Whatsoever you ask in My name—I will give it to you."

"Thou wilt keep him in perfect peace whose mind is stayed on Thee."

"All that I have is yours my son."

"Heaven and Earth shall pass away but My Word shall not."

"Resist the devil and he shall flee from you."

When one is hiking alone far into the wilderness, one is on wild-auto-pilot at all times. This mode of thought is not connected with fear, but with total awareness. The Holy Spirit will warn us of any dangers that may threaten. As with everyday life, authentic Christians relax in the Spirit. We are then also committed to immediate obedience to the Word as it is received.

"Through Christ, Man is in-filled with God's unleashed authority. He trusts, delights, honours and commits to God's gift of grace. It is time for Man to DO. It is time for

Man to BE, for in completeness, "I" and my Father are 'ONE'." (From the Lost Notebooks of Wiser-Mouse).

I AM a Child of Light. With awe and wonderment I project myself into the star-ridden night-skies to galaxies beyond infinity. Spiritual wings transcend light-years to become *NOW*. I am not here, *I AM.*

EPILOGUE

It is difficult to believe that the *Wiser-Mouse Legacy* grew out of a simple week-end Christian retreat. This treatise finally delineates just what I believe it is to be an authentic Christian. It is the spiritual life that Christ initiated for man according to the Scriptures. It enables man to live in love under God's grace, as he prepares himself for the eternity that Jesus promised.

Friends have commented: "Well Derek, you've not revealed to us anything of which we were not already aware. However, you may have identified for some of us, the immense and daunting challenges that face those who would consider being authentic Christians.

What do you recommend for us in the light of the wisdom you have acquired and revealed? The world of religion and spiritual understanding is not going to change just because you were moved to write a book!"

"True" I replied. "But I sincerely believe that any light shed by these words originated with the Holy Spirit, not me. *His Word shall not return void.*"

The *Wiser-Mouse Legacy* may enable men to focus light on their current spiritual comprehension. To live as an authentic Christian, is an individual and very personal spiritual decision. It is simply a matter understanding and applying the principles that Jesus gifted us. It will call for changes to be effected. It is that which God originally intended in order for us to enter the Kingdom.

We have been attempting to introduce a grass-roots concept of change to spiritual authenticity, initiated through the Holy Spirit. We need to experience authentic Christianity.

Authentic Christians are living emulations of Christ, claiming righteousness and Godliness. They are ambassadors for Christ, and the Kingdom. They are engrafted with the Word, and filled with joy! The Word is reflected in their actions, whether by thought, word or deed. God is not mocked; that which man sows is that which he harvests.

In his prayer space, let every reader of the *Legacy,* pray in solitude for any needed changes in his relationship with our heavenly Father, our Lord Jesus Christ and the Holy Spirit.

There is a need for Christians to compare their current practise of Christianity, with that of authentic Christianity. This is attained by referring to the Bible, and conferring with our heavenly Father. God honours the humble. It is written; the Holy Spirit shall guide us, comfort us and lead us in all truth.

We have all questioned the "who, what, when, where and why" of man, or how the cosmos came into being in the first place!

We are intended to dwell within a living prayer, in the presence of the Most High; just as Adam did with God in Eden, after early creation. It is where Godly worship originated.

Often, my spiritual-being stands entranced by the whirl of the galaxies, and the more familiar stars. At times like these, one experiences ecstatic oneness with Earth, the Universe and God. One becomes all that "is", whether it is owls, grizzlies, and mice, or for that matter the river, the trees, the flowers and grasses. It is the bridge of consciousness that merges the worlds of both molecular and ethereal awareness.

We have already determined that Man is a series of levels and states of "being". He *is* his understanding of "time". Truly, only by this perception can a man really be "known". He it is, who controls the *ratio* of his transcendent spiritual time to his earthly-body time.

None of these indescribable inputs of the Spirit are mine alone. Being beyond linguistics, they are Godly gifts of consciousness lovingly unveiled. It is here we experience our *beings* fully alive in spirit, soul and body. I trust that you will have the courage and Godly faith to accept this invitation to explore the world of authentic Christianity.

It is fitting that Wiser-Mouse should have a few final words!

"Men are seeds sown into 'time' by the Son of Man for a specific purpose. In the Godly bloom of spiritual maturity, Man is authorized and fully-empowered to effectively enact the teachings of Jesus." (From the Lost Notebooks of Wiser-Mouse).

My Father is the Father of Lights. The love of God *"IS"*, *"I AM".* Behold! Now the Christian Odyssey takes flight; ascending to the Kingdom!

APPENDICES

Complete "Wiser-Mouse" quotes from the *"Lost Notebooks of Wiser-Mouse"*.

"Truth lived is Godly empowerment. The Holy Scriptures are Man's ultimate guide. When Man has experienced messages from God through the Holy Spirit, and lived them in obedience, it is a record of spiritual reality that can never be forgotten or denied." Ch. 1.

* * * * *

"Natural Man dwells in a spiritual void. He is a living entity of symptoms that proclaim this state. He is both alive, and dead, in time, and in the world of illusion. The solution to his problem is his spiritual awakening. Then only, can he be a complete human being." Ch. 1.

* * * * *

"When Man in the spirit 'comes to himself', his yearning for the Presence of God will be publicly consummated in his Holy Baptism. He will become one with the Body of Christ." Ch. 1.

* * * * *

"The true Christian is indwelt by the Holy Spirit. His church is within his soul. He joins with other Christians whenever and wherever he can. His God-consciousness is unbroken. He is part of the Body of Christ." Ch. 1.

*   *   *   *   *

"Man is beset by feelings of not knowing who he is, or what he is." Ch. 1.

*   *   *   *   *

"The practise of authentic Christianity is that of Man consciously applying the spiritual principles that Christ taught. It is grace-gifted empowerment that unleashes the authority and power of God." Ch. 1.

*   *   *   *   *

"God's throne is established on authority which is synonymous with active faith. Man is the Spirit is the highest expression of God's will." Ch. 1.

*   *   *   *   *

"The state of being Christian requires a degree of withdrawal from the vortices of life that is lived by most of Mankind." Ch. 1.

*   *   *   *   *

"Spiritual leaders with insidious doctrine closely resembling God's truth shall arise in the last days. Man's dangerous mixing of truth with error will be a primary cause of his fallen spiritual state." Ch. 1.

*   *   *   *   *

"Only Man's state of consciousness separates him from God. Oneness with the Father is the state wherein Man transcends himself. In God's Presence he discovers his

naked state-of-being. This is where Man commences his ascension." Ch. 1.

* * * * *

"On the 'key-ring' of life, obedience to God is rooted in the engrafted Word. It is empowered by Faith, and is the only access to Salvation, the Kingdom of God, Heaven and Eternity." Ch. 1.

* * * * *

"Man is absolute purity of spirit may experience oneness with God. Only rarely will his unity with God's Presence peak to the ecstatic state of 'I AM'." Ch. 2.

* * * * *

"Man awakened, needs to become acquainted with his inner-self. He will then observe the activities of his soul, and experience spiritual growth. Under the authority of Christ he becomes a 'Child of Light', impervious to the powers of darkness." Ch. 2.

* * * * *

"Man needs to recognize that he is spirit, soul and body. The Spirit is God-given. The Soul is a living soul. The Body is God-formed." Ch. 2.

* * * * *

"In fear, Man draws a circle of protection around himself to keep love out. In love, God draws a circle around Man, and brings him in!" Ch. 2.

* * * * *

"Man dies internally if he lacks recognition of spiritual values, purpose and direction." Ch. 2.

* * * * *

"In this life, Man can only reach God through love, never by thought or knowledge." Ch. 2.

* * * * *

"Man's failure to abdicate his 'throne of self', negates his spiritual power to 'bring things into being that were not'." Ch. 2.

* * * * *

"The Word of God engrafted in the heart of Man is a fountain of love, trust and peace. Devoid of fear, Man is a beacon of light. He dwells in the parallel worlds of soul and spirit in harmony with God." Ch. 2.

* * * * *

"The greatest demand that God's Word places on Man is for him to obey. Obedience is absolutely honouring God, for it alone acknowledges God's Will at its centre" Ch. 3.

* * * * *

"Throughout life, every word and prayer that Man utters will shape his destiny." Ch. 3.

* * * * *

When miracles occur, Man's loss of 'self' has transpired. It is a 'unity of being' suddenly established, by which God and the spirit of Man become as one." Ch. 3.

"Authority cannot be established in the universe without obedience, since authority cannot exist alone." Ch. 3.

"Empowerment of spiritual authority is released directly in proportion to Man's attained degree of obedience to God's Word. Encompassed by God's authority, it generates the faith-power to achieve miracles." Ch. 3.

"Authority is established to execute God's order. Man is a steward of this authority. As such, he represents God in his every word and action." Ch. 3.

"Intuitive thinking expands Man's thought processes exponentially. It extends far beyond logic. It originates in 'Now', and is spiritual in nature." Ch. 3.

"No man can escape from himself unless he has 'somewhere to go'. The inner-states of Man undergo gradual spiritual evolution." Ch. 3.

"When Man undertakes to bring his life into relationship with God, he embarks upon a serious and demanding task. There is no leeway for self-deception, dream, or illusion." Ch. 3.

"Time is a graveyard of lost souls. Man only truly dies when he fails to discover, or forgets why he was born into this parenthesis in Eternity." Ch. 4.

* * * * *

"When Man elects to replace the Word of God with the word of Man, he has become a power unto himself. He has separated his spirit from God's spirit. Thusly Man sows the seeds of his destruction." Ch. 4.

* * * * *

"Man cannot embrace neutrality through ignorance. It is not possible to be a power unto one's self, and yet claim to worship God." Ch. 4.

* * * * *

"When spiritual Man has no conscious intent, the Universe becomes a state of ecstatic cosmic unity. In this 'I AM' state of being, he experiences the Presence of God." Ch. 4.

* * * * *

"In spiritual solitude Man learns that prayer shapes Eternity. Prayer is the transition of molecular-man to the ethereal indwelling spirit of God's love." Ch. 4.

* * * * *

"To experience is to know. To draw aside the countless veils of consciousness one by one, yields that fragrance which empowers Man to wander among the flowers of Eternity. To see their petals open to the light of 'I AM' Is His spiritual gift." Ch. 5.

*   *   *   *   *

"Man needs to be aware of his sanctified spiritual routes to the kingdoms of God. Only men of Godly intent and the purest spirit of 'I AM' may enter the portals of Eternity." Ch. 5.

*   *   *   *   *

"Man has yet to learn how to enter the Presence of God. He needs to be indwelt by the Holy Spirit and devoid of 'self'. Only then will he be empowered to receive." Ch. 5.

*   *   *   *   *

"Godly contact is a flowing river of spiritual wisdom. Man may navigate these prayer-waters powered only by selfless love, faith and humility. It is here where Man the created, speaks with his Creator." Ch. 5.

*   *   *   *   *

The prayers of authentic Christians rise spontaneously before God. They encompass only the pure intent of their hearts." Ch. 5.

*   *   *   *   *

"Man under the power of sin, without confession, isolates himself from God. In humility he petitions God for forgiveness, in the name of Jesus." Ch. 5.

*   *   *   *   *

"For life to become a living prayer, Man needs an unbroken connection with God. As yet, most of Mankind has to *transition from incompleteness in 'time', to wholeness in the eternal realm." Ch. 5.*

*   *   *   *   *

"Man is exhorted to pray without ceasing. He is endowed with grace and power to achieve this. His prayer-life establishes a living spiritual-bridge with Eternity." Ch. 5.

*   *   *   *   *

"Grace flows from the fountain of God's love. It is Man's indwelt Godly power awaiting his recognition. It empowers him to face all problems. It is Man, in thought, word, and deed, gifting love to man." Ch. 6.

*   *   *   *   *

"Trust is faith in full bloom. Trust is the most felt of all the spiritual qualities. It only works through love. Whereas Hope expects, Trust receives." Ch. 6.

*   *   *   *   *

"Man's indwelt octaves of insight are a series of diatonic degrees of comprehension. In the spiritual acquisition of these degrees, Man creates the celestial-harmonics of 'star-music'." Ch. 6.

*   *   *   *   *

"There is no break in cosmic continuity. God, Man, time and the aeons, are integral with the flow of God's universal design." Ch. 6.

*   *   *   *   *

"Living in faith is Man's act of receiving. It is prayer in motion, powered by trust." Ch. 6.

* * * * *

"Man often believes and acts on that which he has incorrectly comprehended. Therefore, devoid of true understanding, he dwells in a trance-like state of unawareness." Ch. 6.

* * * * *

"Man unawakened is incomplete. He sleeps. Sleep and death are 'time-states of oblivion' that do not exist in Eternity." Ch. 6.

* * * * *

Man's heightened awareness and authority, equates with his ever increasing accountability to the Father." Ch. 6.

* * * * *

"The spiritual word of awakened Man is the instrument that achieves miracles in his mosaic of reality. The Father is thereby glorified." Ch. 6.

* * * * *

"Only Man committed by Christian Baptism will mature into 'Christhood'. It is a life-long spiritual journey." Ch. 6.

* * * * *

"Man, as an authentic son of God is a Child of Light. No element of darkness can penetrate his spiritual raiment. No form of evil can exalt itself above 'I AM', the one true God." Ch. 7.

*   *   *   *   *

"God's covenant with Man is honoured by the act of tithing. It is spiritual stewardship of Man's total resources. Tithing is the evidence of faith expressed. It is an immutable living love-trust." Ch. 7.

*   *   *   *   *

"Through Christ, Man is in-filled with God's unleashed authority. He trusts, delights, honours and commits to God's gift of grace. It is time for Man to DO. It is time for Man to BE, for in completeness. "I" and my Father are 'One'." Ch. 7.

*   *   *   *   *

"Men are seeds sown into 'time' by the Son of Man for a specific purpose. In the Godly bloom of spiritual maturity, Man is authorized and fully-empowered to effectively enact the teachings of Jesus." Epilogue.

*   *   *   *   *

AUTHOR BIOGRAPHY

As a child the author was a small boy who did not have permission to live. In his 2006 book entitled *"Little Boy Wild"* he describes his epic real-life journey as a child in search for himself. His text is fearless, transparent and hauntingly beautiful although sometimes quite disturbing.

Derek was one of four siblings. His background to age sixteen was one typical of toxic highly dysfunctional family life. His trauma of extreme childhood physical brutality, included attempts on his life through suffocation, stabbing and incessant beatings by his mother. He was subjected to sexual abuse, and was raped from an early age. He was strangled and raped by one perpetrator and left for *dead*. These all contributed to his Dissociative Identity Disorder, (multiple personality) scenario.

To escape the torture scene, at age sixteen he left home and worked as a farm labourer in the west of England. He milked cows, sheared sheep, and performed general farm chores. In doing so he experienced the beauty of living fear-free and pain-free for the first time. Compounding his introversion and gross mistrust of humans, his stuttering problem left him crippled and suffering in a negative world of incoherency.

In addition to this, his other personalities in turn controlled him in escapades which were both devastating and alarming. Eventually he went *in search of himself*. So much for the basic Little Boy Wild personality!

Apart from an elementary school education, the author is entirely self-educated. He had no high school, and currently holds no degrees, certificates or educational qualifications in any field of endeavor.

At age twenty he immigrated to Saskatchewan, Canada as a farm worker. Within two years, despite his crippling stutter, through an amazing series of events, he became a radio announcer! A small trucking venture on the side failed miserably.

Later in Alberta, Canada, he experienced a marketing venture as importer and sole distributor of fire extinguishers. In doing so his greatest success was the accumulation of massive debt!

Destitute, heavy with debt and running a vehicle of extreme interest to the authorities; he negotiated a sales position with a U.S. management consulting company. Here he experienced almost instant success. He was promoted to management within two years. He had also now acquired the ability to speak! Several years later he formed his own consulting company. His first book entitled *Management through Commitment* was a product of his management consulting experience.

Eventually he adopted a quieter life-style and became an insurance broker and financial advisor serving rural British Columbia, from which he has only recently retired. He is an avid wilderness dweller and wildlife videographer.

Along life's journey, his painful life traumata and slow Christian progress enabled him to also counsel persons with critically damaged psyches. From practical experience he graduated from the states of being a *victim,* to *survivor,* and finally into *recovery* as an *overcomer.* His passion for authentic Christianity is tracked in the *Wiser-Mouse Legacy.*

Derek is married. He has three sons in professional management in both business and industry. He now lives in the Fraser Valley just outside of Vancouver, British Columbia. Whenever possible, both he and his wife enjoy exploring the wilderness and observing the wildlife.